# BANKING INDUSTRY IN INDIA

# BANKING INDUSTRY IN INDIA

*Edited by*

DR. M. SUMATHY

**REGAL PUBLICATIONS**
New Delhi - 110 027

BANKING INDUSTRY IN INDIA

ISBN 978-81-8484-098-8



*Typeset by*
RAHUL COMPOSERS
358, Pocket-B, Phase-2, Sector-16 B, Dwarka, New Delhi - 110 075

*Printed in India at*
MAYUR ENTERPRISES
WZ Plot No. 3, Gujjar Market, Tihar Village, New Delhi - 110 018

*Published by*
REGAL PUBLICATIONS
F-159, Rajouri Garden, New Delhi - 110 027 • Phone : 45546396
E-mail : regalbookspub@yahoo.com

# Contents

# Preface

I have been looking for an edited book which takes a holistic view of Indian Banking Sector, takes a modern approach to the subject, discusses the traditional as well as emerging models, focuses on intuitive analysis but not at the expense of essential math, and gives a succinct appraisal of the banking environment in India and the world. Though there are many excellent books on Banking and each has its own strengths. This book has, therefore, evolved out of my experience of encouraging the buddy researchers and doctoral students of banking and finance as well as financial executives.

India has a well-developed and distributed banking system with constituents of various size, ownership patterns, geographic locations, business focuses and thrust areas. While the Public Sector Banks (PSB) account for a major part of the total business, the Private Sector Banks, particularly the New Private Sector Banks, are also making significant in roads into the market share, driving the intensity of competition in the domestic banking sector. Some of the foreign banks that have operations in India play a prominent role in the personal and corporate banking segment, accounting for a major part of the off-balance sheet business growth.

In the background of strong economic growth and a deepening financial sector, the opportunity available for Indian banking is enormous. A growing need for financial services in the cities and towns of India presents the banks with a unique opportunity to develop their personal and retail banking spectrum. Focusing on financial inclusion, which became a major policy imperative, will enable banks to penetrate the vast expanse of rural India, where an abundant opportunity for business continues to emerge. Basel II norms bring in the best practices in capital adequacy and risk management. As a result, significant progress in containing the level of non-performing assets would bring about a period of growth and consolidation for Indian banking. While prospects for growth are quite enormous, there is also scope for a continuous evaluation of risks and possible set backs. Global banking today is facing a crisis, brought about by the tribulations in sub-prime loans and structured products. Although innovation is an important aspect of finance, managing risks from sophisticated and riskier.

India is well positioned to become the fourth-largest economy in the world by 2025. GDP growth rates of 7-8 per cent a year will be sustainable going forward if key enabling factors have been put in place. One of the enablers of robust economic growth is a banking sector that is able to adequately and efficiently meet the needs of a growing economy.

It is in this context that I have approached "Indian Banking". We believe that the shape of the banking sector in 2010 will be the result of a strong interplay between the decisions taken by policy madders and actions of bank managements.

The book contains fifteen articles. I have tried to bring the modern concepts of banking sector. I hopes that this document, although by no means a prescription, will help facilitate discussion and debate as both policy-makers and banks progress towards the common objective of creating a world class banking sector in India.

DR. M. SUMATHY

# *List of Contributors*

**Dr. G. Raju**, Reader (UGC Research Awardee 2006-09), Department of Commerce, University of Kerala, Thiruvanathapuram (Kerala).

**Soju, S.**, Lecturer, Department of Commerce, University of Kerala, Thiruvanathapuram (Kerala).

**A. Vasumathi**, SG. Lecturer, VIT Business School, VIT University, Vellore (T.N.).

**Ms. R. Subashini**, Lecturer, VIT Business School, VIT University, Vellore (T.N.).

**C.M. Maran**, Lecturer, VIT Business School, VIT University, Vellore (T.N.).

**Dr. N. Sundaram**, Faculty, Finance and Accounting, VIT Business School, VIT University, Vellore (T.N.).

**Dr. Vijay Pithadia**, Director I/C and Assistant Professor, H.D. Gardi School of Management Studies, Rajkot (Gujarat).

**N. Sumathi**, Lecturer, Department of Commerce, Dr. SNS Rajalakshmi College of Arts and Science, Coimbatore (T.N.).

**J. Jayashree**, Lecturer, Department of Commerce, Dr. SNS Rajalakshmi College of Arts and Science, Coimbatore (T.N.).

**Dr. M. Sumathy**, Reader in Commerce, Bharathiar University, Coimbatore (T.N.).

**Dr. M. Balasundaram**, Reader in Commerce, Government Arts College, Karur (T.N.).

**Dr. M. Basheer Ahmed Khan**, Senior Professor and Head of the Department of Management Studies, Pondicherry University, Puducherry (T.N.).

**Dr. Swaroop Chandra Sahoo**, Former Senior Professor of Department of Business Administration, Utkal University and Director of Bhubaneshwar Institute of Management and Technology, Bhubaneshwar (Orissa).

**Prof. Sheba Sangeetha**, Faculty Member, ICFAI School of Financial Studies (ISFS), 151/90, Lloyds Road, Royapettah, Chennai (T.N.).

**Dr. Rana Zehra Masood**, Lecturer, Department of Commerce, Muslim University, Aligarh (U.P.).

**M. Chandrasekaran**, Assistant Professor, Department of Management Studies, Kathir College of Engineering, Coimbatore (T.N.).

**M.K. Durgamani**, Research Scholar, Department of Commerce, Periyar University, Salem (T.N.).

**S. Uma**, Lecturer, Dept. of Commerce, Dr. SNS Rajalakshmi College of Arts and Science, Coimbatore (T.N.).

**V. Sridevi**, Lecturer in Commerce, Dr. SNS Rajalakshmi College of Arts and Science, Coimbatore (T.N.).

**K. Sumathi**, Lecturer in Commerce, Dr. SNS Rajalakshmi College of Arts and Science, Coimbatore (T.N.).

**M. Sathana Priya**, Research Scholar, Department of Commerce, Bharathiar University, Coimbatore (T.N.).

# 1

# Development of India Warrants a Sustainable University-Industry Linkages

G. Raju

India is emerging as an economic super power and it is expected that Inida will be a developed country in the near future. No less a person than our former President Abdul Kalam has set an agenda for turning India into a developed nation by 2020, urging the industrialists and universities to transform the 'industrial society' into a 'knowledge-powered society'. But the repeated proclamation of politicians and economists and the positive comments from even World Bank have raised expectations that will be difficult to sell. This is because there hardly exists any blue print of how this gargantuan task of raising per capita income from $ 400 to $ 2000 in 12 years can be achieved without worsening the equity aspect.

It is an admitted fact that research has remained the single most important contributor to the growth of all developed countries irrespective of the level from which it started. The emphasis on Research in developed countries is evidenced by its raising investments. This is followed by focussing on sectors such as software, communications, pharmaceuticals, biotechnology and technical innovation in medicine which have the largest spill over effect on growth and development. Given the high capabilities of some Indian firms in these sectors such as Infosys, Natco Pharma, Ranbaxy, etc., any increase in research investment in these sectors is sure to facilitate manufacturing sectors on competing globally.

Another important aspect of this Research and Development is that it led the growth in realising the true potential of University-Industry linkage. The importance of this linkage stems from the fact that research without industry will not create wealth or improve neither the quality of life, nor the industry prosper without academic research.

In this paper, it is attempted to illustrate the present state of University-Industry linkage in India. It also suggests what steps need to be done to strengthen the links that would facilitate realising the dream.

## LINKAGE—PRESNT STATUS

The per capita Research and Development investment and the per capita pool of researchers are the two most important indicators which reflect the state of research and development in any country. On both these angles the picture of India is too pathetic. Against a global annual expenditure on Research and Development of \$ 500-600 billion, India spends a mere \$ 2.5 billion, which is slightly above what Merck, a U.S.-based pharmaceutical firm, spent (\$ 2.1 billion) in 1999.

Realising the positive correlation between investment in research and economic development, the Central Government has openly declared its plan of raising investment in Research to 2 per cent of GDP by the end 2007. From an all-time low Research intensity of 0.71 per cent in 1995-96, the increase to 0.87 percent in 1999-00 is an indication of the growing importance accorded to Research. However, the real fruit of this investment will come only if Research in India becomes more close ended, i.e. it should have more linkages to the end user. This is possible only if the untapped potential of industry-university linkage is more actively harnessed so as to benefit the society at large.

Another characteristic of Indian Research institutions militating against vigorous Research capabilities is the outnumbering of technical manpower by the support staff. Against an average 149 researchers in India for every million population, the three largest spenders on Research—the US, Japan and Germany—have an average 3805 researchers.

The recent past has witnessed a sea change in the ways business is being conducted in India. Consequence of this, any Research strategy must involve all the three legs of the tripod—Universities, Industries and the Government. As of now, because of mutual exclusiveness of their interests, the three players are working without any coordination. Government interest in research is mainly of its strategic or directed type, influenced by defence requirements, public health, environmental issues and similar concerns. Industry's interests are mainly applied in nature whereas Universities channel their efforts and resources in fundamental and unidirectional research. But it is to be noted that some reputed institutions like IITs in India have already gone ahead and firmed up meaningful tie-ups with the industry and some of them are even thinking of starting its own industries following the path Stanford University and the University of California, which had not only created an industry but played an active role in its growth.

## LINKAGE GAP—WHY?

As has been stated earlier, barring a few exceptions like the IITs and private institutions (Shriram Iinstitute in Delhi) Universities in India has no link with the needs of industry. A number of reasons can be cited for this. Important among them are:

- Lack of any industrial experience.
- Choice of research topics based on the interest for the supervisor.
- Publication-oriented research with an eye on publication.
- Outdated research labs and equipments.

Nature of organisation, type of research, aim of research, speed of research, nature of research and research activity are major factors hindering synergies between university and Industrial research. Besides these, lack of effective communication deprives both parties of vital information regarding their respective priorities and capabilities. However, it is to be noted that most of these differences are not insurmountable. The recent trend of curtailing financial support to university and other research labs has made them pro-active in carrying out applied research.

Above all, the word research is interpreted in its narrow sense, i.e. research always implied pure research aimed at finding out how nature works and was considered the monopoly of universities. The outcome of all these is that either there is a complete mismatch between industry's needs and academic research or sometimes industry is unaware of the research going on in the institution. There is no denial of the fact that universities and research centres also lack skills to market their products.

## GAP FILLING

Some of these gaps can easily be bridged if there is a proper interface between industry and academics. Developed countries such as the U.S., the U.K. and France understood the dynamics of this gap and created agencies leading to an effective interface. For instance, CNRS in France, SERC (Scientific and Engineering Research Council) in the U.K. and federal agencies in the U.S. such as NASA have acted in the past and continue to act as an effective interface between industry and academia. A similar interface agency in India can easily bring out the best of the available resources. Both government and industries can submit their problems and research needs to this agency which can identify the most suitable place—a research centre or university or a group of them—where they can entrust the research problem.

Of course, the Gap between university and industry is not specific to India or developing countries. Most Developed countries had this gap in the not-to-too distant past. However, these countries realised that if this gap was not bridged, the end-result would be detrimental to growth. Accordingly, the past 2-3 decades have witnessed the U.S., followed by the U.K. and other OECD countries embarking on an action plan to reduce this gap. It is expected that the following initiatives from industry will go a long way to reduce the gap.

- make an inventorisation of the need, that is, what kind of human resources and skills it would require,
- Provide support for student projects,
- Sponsor long-term research,
- Hold periodic seminars in collaboration with Universities,
- Share equipments and facilities with universities,
- Participate in the teaching by sending industry people as guest faculty,
- Provide scholarships to students at the master's level to take up research, but the sponsored students could not be forced to join a particular company. The company had to look at it as a Corporate Social Responsibility.

Off-load some of the real time projects to the academia:

- Take initiative for partnership models where students, teachers and the industry do research together.
- Participate in faculty development programme.

Simultaneously, some initiatives are needed from the university side also. There is a need to create more design, development, and experiments-oriented curriculum. These include recognising the fact that in today's scenario the needs of industry are totally different. Not only the person needed by industry should have the required qualifications, but he should also have good communication skills and an understanding of how technology links up to economics and the commercial world. More rewarding initiative from the university would be inviting industry to participate in periodic review of syllabi and course content at undergraduate and graduate levels. Besides securing financial support universities can reap many benefits that include making use of sophisticated and expensive industrial equipment and facilities; gaining first hand industrial experience, identifying problems leading to sponsored research projects or consulting opportunities, and attracting students from industry for a continuing education or professional advancement programme.

In brief the Indian education system at present is poor at engagement, does not commercialise research, provide little curricular support to careers in customer contact and innovation, and has limited support for life-long research. Thus to respond the Indian universities to the current business climate, then the action from the Universities needed to support that includes the following:

- Develop courses to up-skill staff in industry for new roles and higher level of skills,
- Make courses in industry-related areas accessible to those in workforce,
- Address the urgent deficit in sales and negotiation skills,
- Evaluate technical skills requirement and respond with relevant curricula,
- Put more emphasis on education in soft skills and attitudes, and
- Continue to support manufacturing skills requirements.

All the above must be achieved in the contest of enhanced engagement between industry and University.

## CONCLUSION

Industry is the single most direct beneficiary of

universities' research programmes. On an average more than 90 per cent of graduates are employed by industry, government or private utilities. This dependence and the direct role of industry in the growth of a nation warrant strengthening its ties with Universities. The amazing rate of advances in both research and technology has resulted in research becoming not only more detailed and specialised but also more expensive. To some, it has led to 'pulverisation' of research that knows more and more about less and less. However, when research becomes useful for practical purposes it metamorphoses to technology and then requires development. Thus, it becomes imperative that scientific research and technological development coalesce to help achieve the aspirations of high growth, wealth creation and improvement in quality of life. Thus the key to success is to bridge the gap between University and industry so that knowledge at the individual level becomes knowledge at the company level, capable of creating Wealth.

## References

Vinish Kathuria, For Stronger Industry—Lab Linkages, *The Hindu Daily*, 19th March, 2004, Thiruvanathapuram.

Rasheed Kappan, Industry, Academia and the bridge to be crossed, *The Hindu Daily*, 6th November, 2007, Thiruvanathapuram.

www.ebooks.com_display.asp

www.jama.ama.org/cgi/content/abstract/289/6/741

# 2

# Commercial Banks in India
## Beyond 2007-08

G. Raju and Soju, S.

India is the largest country in South Asia with a huge financial system characterized by many and varied financial institutions and instruments. Indian banking sector was well developed even prior to its political independence in 1947. There was significant presence of both foreign and domestic banks and well developed stock market. The system expanded rapidly after nationalization of major commercial banks in late 1969 and ranks in the top quarter among developing countries. In the post-nationalisation period there was a rapid expansion of banks in terms of coverage and also in terms of deposit mobilisation. Although banks enjoyed little autonomy as both lending and deposit rates were controlled until the end of the 1980s. Even if nationalisation of banks helped in the spread of banking to the rural and hitherto uncovered areas, the monopoiy granted to the public sector and lack of competition led to overall inefficiency and low productivity.

The financial sector reforms in India began as early as in 1985 with the implementation of the recommendations of the Committee to Review the Working of the Monetary System (Chakravarti, 1985). But the real momentum was given to it in 1992 with the implementation of the recommendations of the Committee on Financial System (CFS) (Narasimham, 1991). Almost all of the recommendations of the CFS have been implemented in a phased manner. In 1998, another committee, viz., the committee on Banking Sector Reforms (BSR) (Narasimham, 1998) was constituted. The recommendations of the BSR committee have also been implemented in a phased manner.

These reforms are expected to have an impact on the operations of banks. With reduced statutory requirements banks will have more funds at their disposal for commercial lending. And interest rate liberalisation is expected to bring flexibility and competition into the banking system. Competition is also infused by opening up banking sector for the private and foreign banks. Along with these flexibilities, certain regulatory reforms are also introduced, which are meant to make banks strong enough to face fluctuations in the economy. Overall, these reforms are aimed at improving the performance of banks.

Apart from these reforms, The Raghuram G. Rajan Committee on financial sector reforms, appointed on August 17, 2007 has argued for pragmatic steps towards establishing ownership-neutral financial institutions in India. It has also advocated privatisation of public sector banks by reducing government's majority stake in the PSU banks while allowing more foreign ownership. Favouring a level-playing field in the financial sector, the committee said the unevenness in the banking system originated from ownership and public sector banks had been lacking in skilled labour and new technologies. The committee has also suggested selling small under-performing PSU banks to another bank or strategic investor, to gain experience with the process and gauge outcomes.

Further, Commercial banks in India are expected to start implementing Basel II norms by 2009. They are expected to adopt the standardised approach for credit risk and the basic indicator approach for operational risk initially. After adequate skills are developed, both at the banks and at the supervisory levels, some banks may be allowed to migrate to the internal rating-based (IRB) approach. At present, banks in India are venturing into non-traditional areas and generating income through diversified activities other than the core banking activities. Strategic mergers and acquisitions are being explored and implemented. With this, the banking sector is currently on the threshold of an exciting phase.

Given this background it is important to measure the efficiency of commercial banks in India. As the banking sector moves towards international prudential standards and operations, the domestic banks have to compete with foreign banks. While efficiency of banks can be measured in various ways, the present study uses Data Envelopment Analysis to measure the relative efficiency of Indian commercial banks.

## OBJECTIVES OF THE STUDY

The objective of this paper is to measure the productive efficiency of Scheduled Commercial Banks in India for the year 2006-07 and to suggest improvements for the financial year 2007-08. The measurement of efficiency was done using Data Envelopment Analysis (DEA). A model had been constructed to show efficiency scores, for four groups of banks, that is, Public sector banks, Old private sector banks, New private sector banks and Foreign banks. The relative efficiency measurement ultimately aims at suggesting potential improvement for each group of banks for the financial year 2007-08.

## METHODOLOGY

There were 88 Scheduled commercial banks in India as on 31$^{st}$ March 2006. Among these 28 banks were in the public sector. There were also 21 old private sector banks, 8 new private sector banks and 31 foreign banks in the country. The overall financial performance of the banking sector improved during 2006-07 as compared with the previous year. Banks were able to increase net interest income. Net profits of banks increased, despite decline in trading profits (due to hardening of sovereign yield) on the one hand, and increase in expenditure and provisions and contingencies, on the other. The measurement of efficiency of Scheduled commercial banks in India was done using Data Envelopment Analysis (DEA). A model had been constructed to show the relative efficiency scores of the four groups of scheduled commercial banks in India. Data had been obtained from REPORT ON TREND AND PROGRESS OF BANKING IN INDIA, 2006-07 published by Reserve Bank of India, Mumbai.

## DATA ENVELOPMENT ANALYSIS

Data Envelopment Analysis (DEA) is a linear programming technique initially developed by Charnes, Cooper and Rhodes (1978) to evaluate the efficiency of public sector non-profit organisations. Sherman and Gold (1985) were the first to apply DEA to banking. DEA calculates the relative efficiency scores of various Decision-Making Units (DMUs) in the particular sample. The DMUs could be banks or branches of banks. The DEA measure compares each of the banks/ branches in that sample with the best practice in the sample. It tells the user which of the DMUs in the sample are efficient and which are not. The ability of the DEA to identify possible peers or role models as well as simple efficiency scores gives it an edge over other methods. As an efficient frontier technique, DEA identifies the inefficiency in a particular DMU by comparing it to similar DMUs regarded as efficient, rather than trying to associate a DMU's performance with statistical averages that may not be applicable to that DMU. DEA modelling allows the analyst to select inputs and outputs in accordance with a managerial focus. This is an advantage of DEA since it opens the door to what-if analysis. Furthermore, the technique works with variables of different units without the need for standardisation (e.g. rupees, number of transactions, or number of staff).

However, DEA has some limitations. When the integrity of data has been violated, DEA results cannot be interpreted with confidence. Another caveat of DEA is that those DMUs indicated as efficient are only efficient in relation to others in the sample. It may be possible for a unit outside the sample to achieve a higher efficiency than the best practice DMU in the sample. Knowing which efficient banks are most comparable to the inefficient bank enables the analyst to develop an understanding of the nature of inefficiencies and re-allocate scarce resources to improve productivity. This feature of DEA is clearly a useful decision-making tool in benchmarking. As a matter of sound managerial practice, profitability measures should be compared with DEA results and significant disagreements investigated.

## THE MODEL

The choice of inputs and outputs in DEA is a matter of long standing debate among researchers. Two approaches exist. One is called the production approach while the other is an intermediation approach.

Although there exists no clear classification of inputs and output factors in the banking production process compared to manufacturing firms, the banking literature can generally be divided into the intermediation approach and the production approach. These two approaches differ in the way they treat deposits in the process; deposits are inputs in the intermediation approach but are considered as output in the production approach.

The production approach characterises banks as producers of services related with loan and deposit accounts. In this approach, the number of loan and deposit accounts are considered as output along with other earning assets. Here following Drake (2001) and Lee and Lee (2001), a modified version of the intermediation approach, which recognises that banks in recent years have increasingly been generating income from off-balance sheet business and fee income is adopted.

The intermediation approach on the other hand considers banks as financial intermediaries and uses volume of deposits, loans and other variables as inputs and outputs. Most of the DEA studies follow an intermediation approach. Within the intermediation approach, the exact set of inputs and outputs used depends largely on data availability. As already stated DEA is sensitive to the choice of input-output variables. This is strength of the technique, since it reveals which of the input-output variables need to be closely monitored by bank management to improve efficiency.

In this study the efficiency has been calculated using variable returns to scale (VRS) input-oriented model of the DEA methodology. To measure efficiency as directly as possible, that is, management's success in controlling costs and generating revenues (that is, x-efficiencies), three input and one output variables, namely, interest expenses, operating expenses, total assets (inputs) and net profit (output) have been used. The input-output specification of this study is outlined in Table 1.

TABLE 1

**Intermediation Model Input-Output Specification**

| | *Banking Variables* |
|---|---|
| Inputs | Interest Expense |
| | Operating Expense |
| | Total Assets |
| Outputs | Net Profit |

## DEA RESULTS

The efficiency of the target bank can be obtained by solving the DEA equations using DEA software. The solution to this LP gives a measure of the relative efficiency of the target bank group and the weights leading to that of efficiency. These weights are the most favourable ones from the point of view of the target bank group. To obtain the efficiencies of the Commercial banks it is necessary to solve the LP focusing on each group inturn. In this study no weightage had been given for any group of banks. The input and output figures of each of the bank group for the year 2006-07 is given in Table 2.

The efficiencies obtained for Public sector banks, Old private sector banks, New private sector banks and Foreign banks were given in Table 3.

### Table 2
## Key Variables of Scheduled Commercial Banks in India

*(Rupees in Crores)*

| *Variables* | *Public Sector Banks* | *Old Private Sector Banks* | *New Private Sector Banks* | *Foreign Banks* |
|---|---|---|---|---|
| Interest Expense (Input) | 103456.63 | 7091.82 | 25801.93 | 7615.02 |
| Operating Expense (Input) | 43254.52 | 2969.17 | 12353.72 | 7741.22 |
| Total Assets (Input) | 2439985.92 | 160561.92 | 584842.08 | 278016.49 |
| Net Profit (Output) | 20152.18 | 1121.87 | 5343.40 | 4585.16 |

*Source* : Report of Trend and Progress of Banking in India, 2006-07.

### Table 3
## Efficiency Scores of Commercial Banks in India

| *Bank* | *Efficiency Score* |
|---|---|
| Public sector banks | 78.66 |
| Old private sector banks | 63.79 |
| New private sector banks | 73.03 |
| Foreign banks | 100.00 |

*Source* : Computed Values.

For the year 2006-07, foreign banks shows relatively high efficiency score and Old private sector banks shows the least efficiency (only 63.79). Public sector banks had a comparatively better score of 78.66 and new private sector banks had a score of 73.03. Importantly, it is to be noted that foreign banks is the peer group. The following Tables show the potential improvement of other group of banks for the next year.

It is evident from Table 4 that the public sector banks have to reduce its interest expense by 67.65 per cent, operating expense by 21.34 per cent and total assets by 49.92 per cent to justify its current year net profit. Otherwise, it has to earn more net profit to optimize its interest expense, operating expense and total assets. However, the efficiency score of 78.66 clearly indicates its productive efficiency

TABLE 4

**Efficiency Report of Public Sector Banks**

| *Variable* | *Actual* (2006-07) (Rs. in crores)* | *Target** (Rs. in crores)* | *Potential Improvement** (In per cent)* |
|---|---|---|---|
| Interest expense | 103456.63 | 33468.68 | -67.65 |
| Operating expense | 43254.52 | 34023.34 | -21.34 |
| Total Assets | 2439985.92 | 1221906.84 | -49.92 |
| Net Profit | 20152.18 | 21523.87 | 00.00 |

*Source* : *Report of Trend and progress of banking in India, 2006-07.
**Computed Values.

TABLE 5

**Efficiency Report of Old Private Sector Banks**

| *Variable* | *Actual* (2006-07) (Rs. in crores)* | *Target** (Rs. in crores)* | *Potential Improvement** (In per cent)* |
|---|---|---|---|
| Interest expense | 7091.82 | 1863.20 | -73.73 |
| Operating expense | 2969.17 | 1894.08 | -36.21 |
| Total Assets | 160561.92 | 68023.44 | -57.63 |
| Net Profit | 1121.87 | 1121.87 | 00.00 |

*Source* : *Report of Trend and Progress of Banking in India, 2006-07.
**Computed Values.

The old private sector banks had the least efficiency score of 63.79 per cent in the present input minimization DEA model. This calls for the reduction of interest expense by 73.73 per cent, operating expense by 36.21 per cent and total assets by 57.63 per cent.

The New private sector banks showed the efficiency score of 73.03 which was lower than that of the public sector banks. However, while comparing to the peer group (Foreign banks)

TABLE 6
**Efficiency Report of New Private Sector Banks**

| *Variable* | *Actual** *(2005-06)* *(Rs. in crores)* | *Target*** *(Rs. in crores)* | *Potential Improvement*** *(In per cent)* |
|---|---|---|---|
| Interest expense | 25801.93 | 8874.30 | -65.61 |
| Operating expense | 12353.72 | 9021.37 | -26.97 |
| Total Assets | 584842.08 | 323991.6 | -44.60 |
| Net Profit | 5343.40 | 4108.85 | 00.00 |

*Source* : *Report of Trend and progress of banking in India 2005-06.
**Computed Values.

it has to minimize its interest expense by 54.82 per cent, operating expense by 10.87 per cent, and total assets by 35.99 per cent.

## CONCLUSION

Indian banking sector saw significant change with respect to policy environment after financial sector reforms were introduced in 1992. These reforms are expected to affect the operations of commercial banks. At present, banks in India are venturing into non-traditional areas and generating income through diversified activities other than the core banking activities. Strategic mergers and acquisitions are being explored and implemented. Further, the Indian commercial Banks have to migrate into the new international prudential standard BASEL 2. With this, the banking sector is currently on the threshold of an exciting phase. Thus the present study attempts to measure efficiency of Indian commercial banks for the year 2006-07. The cost minimization variable returns to scale DEA model developed for the study identified foreign Banks as the peer group among the commercial banks working in India. More importantly, the old private sector banks had the least efficiency score. The potential improvement through cost minimization is also suggested in this study. However, the study is only indicative to the regulators and stakeholders to improve their performance in the coming years through policy decisions.

## Rferences

Bhattacharya, A., Lovell, C.A.K., and Sahay, P., 1997: "The impact of liberalization on the productive efficiency of Indian commercial banks", *European Journal of Operational Research*, 98, 332-45.

Chatterjee, G., 1997: "Scale Economies in Banking: Indian Experience in Deregulated Era", *RBI Occasional Papers*, Vol. 18, No. 1, 25-59.

Coelli, T., 1996: A Guide to DEAP Version 2.1, A Data Envelopment Analysis (Computer) Program. *CEPA Working Paper*, 96/08.

Ramanathan, M., 2003: "An Introduction to Data Envelopment Analysis", Sage Publications, New Delhi.

Saha, A., and T.S. Ravishankar, 2000: Rating of Indian Commercial Banks: A DEA Approach, *European Journal of Operations Research*, 124, 187-203.

Keshari, Pradeep K. and M. Thomas Paul (1994): "Relative Efficiency of Foreign and Domestic Banks", *Economic and Political Weekly*, February 26.

Kumar, S. and Satish Verma (2003): "Technical Efficiency, Benchmarking and Targets: A Case Study of Indian Public Sector Banks", *Prajnan*, Vol. XXI, No. 4, 275-311.

Narasimham, M. (1991): "Report of the Committee on the Financial System", Reserve Bank of India, Mumbai.

Narasimham, M. (1998): "Report of the Committee on Banking Sector Reforms", Reserve Bank of India, Mumbai.

——— (2007): "Report on Trend and Progress of Banking in India", Reserve Bank of India, Mumbai.

# 3

# A Competitive Strategy and IT-based Innovations in Banking Services

A. VASUMATHI, MS. R. SUBASHINI AND C.M. MARAN

## ABSTRACT

This article focuses the dynamic relationships between competitive strategies and Information Technology (IT)-based product and process innovation in financial services. The authors have discussed about the IT-based innovations of Inter-branch online service, Automated Teller Machine Service and Mobile Banking benefits. This research explores the limitations of the Reverse Product Cycle model approach, and an alternative conceptual framework and country specific innovation model are proposed. Possible avenues for further research on innovation in services and service innovation are suggested, together with steps towards developing a unified approach to innovation and competition for both the service and manufacturing functions.

## INTRODUCTION

This research focuses the interaction between service innovations and competition through different stages of innovation processes. The second section examines the Reverse Product Cycle model, which has been proposed as a general theory of innovation in services. The third section sets out an alternative *Dynamic Interdependence of Innovation and Competition (DIIC)* framework. The fourth section considers empirical evidence concerning the development of electronic banking services in India.

## THE REVERSE PRODUCT CYCLE MODEL REVISITED

Most innovation research has been concerned with the manufacturing sector, with much less attention paid to the service sectors (Freeman, 1994), and very little examination of the linkage between technology-based service innovation and corporate strategies in changing competitive environments (Brown, 1991; Philip *et al.*, 1995; Schroeder, 1990; Utterback, 1994). In pioneering contributions to research on innovation in services, Barras (1986b; 1990) proposed a general theory of innovation in services—the "Reverse Product Cycle" (RPC)—developed in the course of Barras's research during the early 1980s. His studies focused on the adoption and impact of information technologies (IT) in information-intensive services within the United Kingdom—including insurance, accountancy and local government (Barras, 1983; 1984; 1985). The presumed applicability of the RPC model to the banking sector (Barras, 1990) was, in contrast, based on literature review and conceptual discussion. The present study addresses empirical weaknesses in the RPC approach, studying the banking sector, in a non-UK context.

In the RPC model, innovation in services is determined by the application of new process technologies developed in, and following the technical trajectories of manufacturing sectors; as a result, learning processes become the most crucial factor in determining the accommodation and utilisation of IT in services. Barras argued that innovation in services is not only driven by the technological trajectory of manufacturing sectors; it operates in a "reverse" pattern with respect to the manufacturing-based industrial innovation model, proposed by Abernathy and Utterback (1975; 1978). The RPC model proposes that the innovation process in services generally proceeds through three stages: (i) incremental process innovations which emphasise efficiency improvement, (ii) radical process innovation in pursuit of quality enhancement, (iii) radical product innovations involving "entirely new services" (Table 1). Barras predicted that further development in new services (from stage 3) will simply follow a normal product cycle—i.e. moving from product innovations to radical and incremental process innovations, as often observed in the capital goods sector.

Barras's RPC model has been widely recognised as making an important contribution to easing the shortage of studies of innovation in services. There has to date been little challenge to this model's underlying assumptions and concepts, nor to its applicability in different service sectors in other national contexts (e.g. Buzzacchi *et al.*, 1995). Despite a considerable degree of conceptual criticism of the RPC model (e.g. Gallouj, forthcoming; Hauknes, 1996; Miles, 1993; Thomas and Miles, 1989), there has been little attempt to assess the validity of the RPC model through further empirical research, especially involving historical analysis covering an extensive period. The RPC model sees innovation in services as inherently taking a different pattern from those observed in the goods producing sectors. Thus, Barras interprets results of his studies of the adoption and impact of IT as if they apply exclusively to services. But key features might be shared with the manufacturing sector—both service and manufacturing organisations are IT users, and IT is used to improve process efficiency or product quality in manufacturing firms (Campbell-Kelly, 1996; Friedman, 1989); learning processes in IT implementation are evident in both sectors (Earl, 1989); and exploiting new IT in the 1990s has provided windows of opportunity for both service and manufacturing firms to enter new markets. But beyond such criticisms of the perceived dichotomy between manufacturing and services, how far does the RPC model accurately explain the stages of product/ process innovation and underlying competitive emphases in

TABLE 1

**Barras's Reverse Product Cycle Model**

| *Stage of Cycle* | *1960–1970s* | *1980s* | *1990s Onwards* |
|---|---|---|---|
| *(1)* | *(2)* | *(3)* | *(4)* |
| Innovative characteristics | Incremental process innovation | Radical process innovation | Product innovation |
| Competitive emphases | Efficiency improvement | Quality enhancement | New service realisation |
| Technological innovation in IT producer sectors | Mainframe computers | Online systems; minis and micros, dumb and intelligent | Networking (particularly ISDN) |
| Sector Applications | 1960–1970s | 1980s | 1990s Onwards |
| Retail banking | Automated transactions and financial records | ATMs, financial customer/information systems | Cashless shopping (EPOS) home banking |
| Insurance | Computerised policy records | Online policy quotations | Complete online service |
| Accountancy | Computer audit; internal time recording | Computerised management accounting | Fully automated audit and accounts |
| Local government | Corporate financial systems (e.g. payroll) | Departmental service delivery (e.g. housing allocation) | Public information services (e.g. view data |

*Source* : Adapted from Barras (1986; 1990).

service industries (including banking), in the UK and in other countries? Four sets of problematic assumptions can be identified.

**First, is this a micro or macro theory of innovation in services—or neither?**

The RPC approach is not a micro-economic theory of innovation in services of the (reverse) product life cycle in the marketing sense. [It features no close scrutiny of the degree of market penetration and customer acceptance regarding a service product in the market (Kotler, 1980).] Nor is it one in terms of being a micro-level innovation theory. [It does not examine the innovation process within a particular firm (Ingham *et al.*, 1993; Rogers, 1993), or even deal with an innovation process of a specific service amongst various firms in an industry]. Neither is the model a macro-model of the industry life cycle of a service sector, such as banking or transportation industries—if so, it would discuss the birth, growth, decline and demise or, perhaps, regeneration of any service industry in a particular national context or in the international system. In keeping with the analytical level of the Abernathy and Utterback's industrial innovation model, the RPC model mainly attempts to offer a general explanation of the adoption of IT in specific service industries (e.g. insurance), identifying the types of IT that firms utilised and their competitive emphases.

In other words, the model focuses on explaining how only one source of innovation in service firms—information technologies—was used through time. But despite its limited empirical foundation, the model has been treated as a general account of innovation in services, regardless of differences in functions, organisations, and social contexts.

**Second, is a rigid product-process dichotomy sustainable?**

The RPC model is fundamentally characterised by the assumption that process and product innovations in services are intrinsically separate and occur at different times. However, it can be argued that service product and process are coexisting and inextricably intertwined in complex ways (Bateson, 1977; Grönroos, 1978; Miles, 1987). The RPC model does not examine the extent to which a service product innovation may be developed together with a service process innovation, from the very beginning of the IT-based innovation process. It is not constructed to examine whether and how product and process aspects of service innovations can emerge in parallel. The product–process dichotomy allows the RPC model to emphasize the effect of a learning curve from the early to the later stages of IT use—i.e. from incremental to radical process innovation, and eventually to new product realization.

**Third, What is a New Service?**

The RPC model is intended to distinguish the innovation process in services from that of manufacturing, and attempts to explain the interaction of the two processes. A strict definition of "entirely new services" lies at the heart of the model, being used as a key concept to mark the end of the reverse pattern, in line with Abernathy and Utterback's (1975; 1978) normal industrial innovation model. Barras (1986; 1990) saw the third stage of the process as one in which new technological opportunities from the IT producer sectors would drive service firms to generate "entirely new services" to open up and capture new markets, in parallel with the emergence of new or diversified service industries and organisations. In terms of the service marketing literature (e.g. Cowell, 1989), Barras's "entirely" new services implicitly referred to the level of "service class" 3—e.g. the significant transformation or at least the extension of the boundary of retail banking services. His underlying logic was that the development of an entirely new service, assisted by IT, could be possible only if the continuity of technological learning in service firms became sufficiently mature. [However, there are other factors (e.g. new recruitment of IT experts) which may allow service firms to leap ahead in knowledge accumulation].

Ironically, the examples of new services given by Barras himself; e.g. EFTPOS and Home Banking Services (Table 1), are not compatible with his own definition of "entirely new services". These only fulfil the traditional functions of banking services—e.g. financial transaction and information services—and are still performed by the existing structure of commercial banks. To be faithful to the Barras' own definition of a new service, therefore, the model should have located these services in Stage 2 (i.e. as quality enhancement), instead of Stage 3 (i.e. as new services). In contrast, the ATM service (first introduced in the 1980s) was treated by Barras (1990) as simply a quality improvement in existing services—though it can be argued that this is also a major product innovation. The judgment as to what constitutes new services is based on the views of one innovation researcher, not on the perceptions of customers and service providers themselves. The RPC model would not have been constructed had Barras accepted that the quality improvement and the introduction of new services can take place simultaneously, rather than being necessarily at different innovation stages.

**Fourth, how far are competitive strategies technology-driven?**

The RPC model is not only technologically deterministic, but also fundamentally IT-centric, since it assumes that all service sectors similarly adopt and utilise information technology in their core technological applications, and thus inevitably follow the reverse product cycle. This view does not reflect the fact that service sectors and firms are intrinsically heterogeneous and complex in their service activities and organisational characteristics as well as in technological utilisation (Belleflamme *et al.*, 1986; Miles, 1987). Hence, they can employ either similar or different core technologies (e.g. biotechnology, materials technology and IT) and, in many cases, utilise a combination of several technologies for their distinctive service processes (consider, e.g. hospitals). We can expect to observe several technological trajectories in a service, even in a single firm; and there could be more than one vanguard service based on different uses of advanced technologies, apart from the financial and business services which were designated as such by Barras (1990).

The RPC model portrays service firms as being passive recipients of innovation from the IT producer sectors. Thus, the competitive emphases behind the use of IT in service firms are determined by the generic purposes of technological applications. It sees service firms as typically adopting mainframe computers to improve the efficiency of their production processes during the 1960s and 1970s, mini- and micro-computers along with limited online systems to enhance quality of service product during the 1980s, and (if sophisticated network infrastructure is available) using these to introduce ranges of entirely new services in the 1990s. The RPC model claims that efficiency improvement was the dominant competitive emphasis in the early period of IT use: new services introduced in the 1970s are not seen as having been assisted by this early IT use. In contrast, it does see the new services introduced in the 1990s as growing out of corporate

Data-processing systems—overlooking the association of these new services with IT-facilitated efficiency and quality improvement. Again, the model ignores the scope for service firms to use IT to simultaneously improve service process efficiency and service product quality, and to introduce new services.

More generally, this account ignores the active and dynamic roles of such socio-economic factors as protectionist policies, financial deregulation, and oligopolistic large firms. Further, service firms make their own strategies for developing new IT-based services in the light of their capabilities and competitive environments (Freeman, 1994; Pettigrew, 1985). These and other factors shape the service innovation process in what may be historically specific ways in different firms, industries and national contexts (Miles, 1987; Nelson, 1991; Porter, 1980; Porter, 1990; Schroeder, 1990).

## The Dynamic Interdependence of Innovation and Competition (DIIC) Framework

An alternative framework for the study of innovation and competition, in general, and the dynamics of competitive strategy and service innovation process, in particular, should emphasise the dynamism and complexity of processes, and break with linear, static, fragmented and technologically deterministic approaches to innovation and competition. The Dynamic Interdependence of Innovation and Competition (DIIC) framework is set out below, addressing the dynamics of: (i) services, (ii) service innovation, (iii) innovation process, and

(iv) competitive strategies. The key features of the proposed framework are summarised in Table 2.

TABLE 2

**Four Interdependent Aspects of the DIIC Framework**

| | *Key Features of the DIIC Framework* |
|---|---|
| (1) Dynamics of services | 1.1 Continuum between goods and service products |
| | 1.2 Interdependence and convergence of service and manufacturing activities |
| | 1.3 Heterogeneity and peculiarities of services, changing over time |
| | 1.4 Multiple levels of services and market segments, requiring specification of the level under discussion |
| | 1.5 Interdependence of service product and process in relation to specific service levels |
| | 1.6 Interaction between service activities and technological applications |
| | 1.7 Active roles of services in using, promoting and generating new technology |
| (2) Dynamics of service innovation | 2.1 Significance of interactive, processual, systemic, organisational, and marketing aspects of "innovation", changing over time |
| | 2.2 The coupling of firm- and industry-level factors on innovation characteristics |
| | 2.3 Interdependence of product and process innovation |
| | 2.4 Complex mix of technological and managerial process innovation |
| | 2.5 Active blend of goods and service product innovation |
| | 2.6 Flexible perspective on "new service", with respect to service levels |
| | 2.7 Customers' and managers' perceptions as defining what are new services within specific contexts |

TABLE 2 (*Contd.*)

| | |
|---|---|
| | 2.8 Differences and cycle of radical and incremental innovations recognised |
| (3) Dynamics of innovation process | 3.1 An innovation process as unit of analysis |
| | 3.2 International or country-specific research on each innovation process |
| | 3.3 Interactive intra-industrial innovation and diffusion process |
| | 3.4 Product life cycle-based stages of innovation process |
| | 3.5 Interdependent rate of product/process innovation during the process |
| | 3.6 Interaction between innovation, imitation and competition, driving the innovation process |
| | 3.7 Dynamic innovators and innovatory mobility |
| | 3.8 Complementarity and competition between different innovation processes |
| (4) Dynamics of competitive strategy | 4.1 Eclecticism of competitive strategy |
| | 4.2 Firms and inter-firms diversity in an intra-industrial innovation process |
| | 4.3 Firms as choice makers in an intra-industrial innovation process |
| | 4.4 Interlink between firms' decision and socio-technical contextual factors |
| | 4.5 Leaders as constrained decision-makers in complex settings |
| | 4.6 Perception of firms' managers as a key source of empirical evidence |
| | 4.7 Impact of strategic choice and position on the level of innovativeness that is sought |
| | 4.8 Interaction of multiple strategies within and amongst multiple innovation processes |

The DIIC framework can:

(i) Advance an integrated approach to innovation for both service and manufacturing functions (in contrast to the traditional dichotomy of these two functions). Thus, we can consider service innovation within manufacturing firms (where service innovation complements the total production system and has become critical to competitive success), and manufacturers who have entered service markets (such as General Electric's leasing and credit card businesses). [Based on Features 1.1, 1.2 and 1.3 of the DIIC framework.]

(ii) Illuminate the multiple sources of innovation and technological applications (not only IT) in service innovations in both service and manufacturing organisations. [Features 1.1, 1.2, 1.3, 1.6, 1.7, 2.4 and 2.5.]

(iii) Bridge firm-level and industry-level analyses, and accommodate the dynamic diversity and subtlety in different innovative activities, discretionary organisations, distinctive industry-specific and social contexts. Within the framework, we can examine over time changing components of the activities in which a service firm is involved in the light of organisational, regulatory, marketing and technological potentials. [Features 2.2, 3.3, 3.6, 3.8, 4.2, 4.3 and 4.4.]

(iv) Capture the interaction of innovation and competition through the interdependent evolution of product and process innovations—providing opportunities to identify common innovation trajectories across different technological–managerial systems, or different trajectories dominating or overlapping with one another during an industry life cycle. [Features 2.3, 3.4, 3.6, 3.7, 3.8, 4.7 and 4.8.]

(v) Allow for the possibility that competitive strategies underlying innovation processes are innovation-specific, country-specific, industry-specific or firm specific, proceeding in various ways (even following the RPC model). [Features 1.3, 1.4, 1.5, 2.1, 2.2, 2.6, 2.7, 3.2 and 4 (Dynamics of Competitive Strategy)].

## THE DEVELOPMENT OF ELECTRONIC BANKING SERVICES IN INDIA

We need to learn a great deal more about the historical features of technology-based service innovation, including IT-based banking innovations, in order to test the validity of the RPC model in different country-specific industrial contexts. The Indian banking industry is the setting through which empirical evidence will be derived and key issues discussed in this paper. The country and the industry constitute a unique context in which to consider the applicability of the RPC model.

## INTERNET BANKING

Internet banking provides clients with real-time information about their accounts, and the ability to transfer funds between their accounts. It is an empowering tool because it gives bank clients the flexibility to manage their financial resources deliberately, at their own leisure, and without having to visit a bank office during opening hours. In particular, it is a vital accompaniment to card-based services, allowing clients to keep track of numerous small electronic transactions.

From the bank perspective, Internet banking is an efficiency tool because it reduces the work of (human) tellers and therefore reduces labour costs. It is a relatively easy and inexpensive service to offer, and the incremental cost of having 1.000, 10.000, or 100.000

## INTERNET BANKING CLIENTS IS NEGLIGIBLE

### ATM

ATM is an automatic teller machine which is used to save the cost and reachability of a bank by satisfying customer needs. Customers can withdraw and deposit money without any paper work and it facilitates them to reduce time and cost to go to bank in person. Two types of ATMs need to be addressed, one of which is the branch ATM, the other being the out-of-branch ATM. The branches will take care of the ATM located in their respective branches, while the out-of-branch ATMs such as those located in department store will be taken care by cash centers. Each cash center has ATMs under its responsibility.

### Mobile Banking

Internet Banking helped give the customer's anytime access to their banks. Customer's could check out their account details, get their bank statements, perform transactions like transferring money to other accounts and pay their bills sitting in the comfort of their homes and offices. However, the biggest limitation of Internet banking is the requirement of a PC with an Internet connection, not a big obstacle if we look at the US and the European countries, but definitely a big barrier if we consider most of the developing countries of Asia like China and India. Mobile banking addresses this fundamental limitation of Internet Banking, as it reduces the customer requirement to just a mobile phone. Mobile usage has seen an explosive growth in most of the Asian economies like—

#### *India, China and Korea*

The main reason that Mobile Banking scores over Internet Banking is that it enables 'Anywhere Anytime Banking'. Customers don't need access to a computer terminal to access their bank accounts, now the can do so on-the-go while waiting for the bus to work, traveling or when they are waiting for their orders to come through in a restaurant.

Mobile banking might save the government and banks money and reduce fraud that plagues the public-distribution system.

Mobile phones are making life better for people in remote, underserved areas of India. They no longer have to walk kilometers to public call offices to use a telephone—an essential tool for buying and selling goods based on the latest market data, getting credit from lenders and other commonplace activities. So far, most of the benefits have come from one of the phone's simplest features: voice calls. With more than 250 million mobile users and 6 million new ones added each month, India now has the "tele density" to support more-sophisticated mobile technologies, which could have a big impact on Indian society and the economy in the next few years. (An extra 10 mobile phones per 100 people in a typical developing country leads to an additional 0.59 percentage points of growth in GDP per person, according to a London Business School study.) These include "voice broadcast" services that would let a truck owner inform residents of a village about a scheduled trip to the city, or doctors announce the availability of polio vaccinations. A more complex system would allow a small business, say, to keep track of shipments. What's holding up these services is the lack of mobile banking. With urban markets nearing saturation, global giants like Nokia are now looking to appeal to the hinterlands. Reliance Communications, which has offered Internet service over its mobile phones since 2002, is sponsoring a contest this year for developers to invent new rural services. "We want to really take advantage of our mobile platform, our data network, and our ability to provide the mobile Internet experience to bridge the digital divide," says Mahesh Prasad, president of applications and development.

Several small companies are at work on mobile banking for small businesses. New Delhi-based ekgaon technologies has developed a system for tracking transactions made by so-called Self Help Groups, which pool members' money and offer small loans to poor people. The system uses a camera-equipped mobile phone to scan forms and a voice-recognition system. A.Little.World, a mobile software business in Mumbai, has developed a microfinance and payment system that lets customers perform banking transactions through a local agent affiliated with a bank (a practice allowed for the first time in January 2006). Customers get a secure electronic identity via phone or smart card; agents take deposits and dispense cash. Biometric data, such as fingerprints, make the phones and smart cards more secure than paper-based banking. A.Little.World has extended such services to about 400 local businesses acting as agents. And it's now working on a national rollout with the State Bank of India—the biggest player in the rural market. Meanwhile, ekgaon, whose partners include CARE, World Vision and the World Bank, has a pilot transaction management system for 10,000 Self Help Groups, with plans to extend it to 14 Indian states.

Mobile banking services can reduce the cost of transactions for loans and other services—the main obstacle to providing banking for the poor—by as much as three quarters, according to ekgaon's chief operating officer Rohit Magotra. Mobile transactions could have an even broader effect applied to India's social-security payments and public-distribution system, which sells essential goods to the poor at subsidized rates. By March 2008, people in 8,000 villages in Andhra Pradesh received their benefits zapped via mobile phone to their smart cards, which they may eventually use instead of cash to buy goods at the ration shop. A.Little.World, which is building the system, says a nationwide service could help reduce fraud in the public-distribution system. It would also mean going from a bank less world to a cashless one, maybe even faster than America or Europe.

## Mobile Banking Services

Banks offering mobile access are mostly supporting some or all of the following services:

### *Account Information*

- Mini-statements and checking of account history
- Alerts on account activity or passing of set thresholds
- Monitoring of term deposits
- Access to loan statements
- Access to card statements
- Mutual funds/equity statements
- Insurance policy management
- Pension plan management

### *Payments and Transfers*

- Domestic and international fund transfers
- Micro-payment handling

- Mobile recharging
- Commercial payment processing
- Bill payment processing

### Investments

- Portfolio management services
- Real-time stock quotes
- Personalized alerts and notifications on security prices

### Support

- Status of requests for credit, including mortgage approval, and insurance coverage
- Check (cheque) book and card requests
- Exchange of data messages and email, including complaint submission and tracking

### Content Services

- General information such as weather updates, news
- Loyalty-related offers
- Location-based services

One way to classify these services depending on the originator of a service session is the 'Push/Pull' nature. 'Push' is when the bank sends out information based upon an agreed set of rules, for example, your banks sends out an alert when your account balance goes below a threshold level. 'Pull' is when the customer explicitly requests a service or information from the bank, so a request for your last five transactions statement is a Pull-based offering.

The other way to categorize the mobile banking services, gives us two kind of services—Transaction-based and Enquiry-based. So a request for the bank statement is an enquiry-based service and a request for your fund's transfer to some other account is a transaction-based service. Transaction-based services are also differentiated from enquiry-based services in the sense that they require additional security across the channel from the mobile phone to the banks data servers.

Based upon the above classifications, we arrive at the following taxonomy of the services listed before.

| | *Push-based* | *Pull-based* |
|---|---|---|
| Transaction-based | | • Fund Transfer<br>• Bill Payment<br>• Other financial services like share trading |
| Enquiry-based | • Credit/Debit Alerts<br>• Minimum Balance Alerts<br>• Bill Payment Alerts | • Account Balance Enquiry<br>• Account Statement Enquiry<br>• Cheque Status Enquiry<br>• Cheque Book Requests<br>• Recent Transaction History |

### Technologies Behind Mobile Banking

Technically speaking most of these services can be deployed using more than one channel. Presently, Mobile Banking is being deployed using mobile applications developed on one of the following four channels.

1. IVR (Interactive Voice Response)
2. SMS (Short Messaging Service)
3. WAP (Wireless Access Protocol)
4. Standalone Mobile Application Clients

## CONCLUSION

More and more non banking institutions are going to provide the banking functions than the designated banks in the coming century. Banks are going to be vanished from its existing strong positions. Financial liberalization, internationalization and technological advancement are going to further pressurize the banks to make their struggle for existence. If a bank overcome all these pressures survival of the fittest comes again because of the technological innovation and the type of competition in the banking industry.

For effective financial services and to retain the customers in the market, Banks need to revitalize their fee income flows to supplement and supplant if necessary their net interest margin for which they are required to reemphasis risk management on a daily basis. Banks are forced to give up isolated approaches to the challenges of competition profitably and risk management. Strategic planning has superseded the isolated approaches. The need for sound conceptual and technical skills has been seared into every banker's mind. For banks to survive profitable they have to improve the operational methods with latest hi-tech financial modelling content.

## References

Abernathy, W.J. and Utterback, J.M. (1978) Patterns of industrial innovation. *Technology Review*, 80(7) 40–47.

Athanassopoulos, A.D. (1997) Service quality and operating efficiency synergies for management control in the provision of financial services: evidence from Greek bank branches. *European Journal of Operational Research*, 98(2), 300-13.

Barras, R. (1983) *The Adoption and Impact of Information Technology in the UK Insurance Industry*, London: The Technical Change Centre, Research Report TCCR-83-016.

———, (1985) *The Adoption and Impact of Information Technology in UK Local Government*. London: The Technical Change Centre, Research Report TCCR-83-005.

———, (1986a) New technology and the new services. *Futures*, 18(6), 748–71 (1986b) Towards a theory of innovation in services. *Research Policy*, 15, 161-73.

———, (1990) Interactive innovation in financial and business services: the vanguard of the service revolution. *Research Policy*, 19, 215-37.

Barras, R. and Swann, J. (1984) Information technology and the services sector: Quality of services and quantity of jobs. In *New Technology and the Future of Work and Skills*, ed. P. Marstrand. London: Frances Pinter.

Bessant, J. *et al*. (1994) Rediscovering continuous improvement. *Technovation*, 14(1), 17-29.

Bateson, J. (1977) *Do We Need Service Marketing? Marketing Consumer Services: New Insights*, Report 77-115, November. Boston: Marketing Science Institute.

Belleflamme, C.J. *et al.* (1986) *Innovation and Research and Development Process Analysis in Service Activities,* FAST Occasional Paper No. 116, EC, Brussels, September 1986.

*Competition and IT-based Innovation in Banking Services,* 487.

Benest, I. (1997) The specification and presentation of online lectures. *Innovation In Education And Training International,* 34(1), 32–43.

Blumberg, D.F. (1994) Strategies for improving field service operation productivity and quality. *Service Industries Journal,* 14(2), 262–77.

Brown, R. (1991) Managing the S curves of innovation. *Journal of Marketing Management,* 7, 189–202.

Buzzacchi, L., Colombo, M.G. and Mariotti, S. (1995) Technological regimes and innovation. In services: the case of the Italian banking industry. *Research Policy,* 24, 151-68.

Campbell-Kelly, M. (1989) *ICL: A Business and Technical History.* Oxford: Clarendon Press, Collier, D.A. (1995) Modelling the relationship between process quality errors and overall service process performance. *Journal of Service Industries Management,* 6(4), 4.

Cooper, R.G. (1988) The new product process: a decision guide for management. *Journal of Marketing Management,* 3(3), 238–55.

Cooper, R.G. and de Brentani, U. (1991) New industrial financial services: what distinguishes the winners. *Journal of Product Innovation Management,* 8, 75-90.

Cowell, D. (1988) New service development. *Journal of Marketing Management,* 3(3), 296-312.

———, (1989) *The Marketing of Services.* The Marketing Series, London: The Institute of Marketing.

Credé, A. (1996) *Technological Change and the Information Society—An Examination of Credit Risk Assessment and Cash Handling Procedures in Commercial Banks.* Unpublished Ph.D. Dissertation, University of Sussex, Brighton.

Currie, W. (1994) The strategic management of a large scale IT project in the financial services sector. *New Technology, Work and Employment,* 9(1), 19-29.

Donnelly, M. (1996) Setting standards for reception services in UK local authorities. *Total Quality Management,* 7(1), 51-66.

Dosi, G. (1988) Sources, procedures, and micro-economic effects of innovation. *Journal of Economic Literature,* 16, 1120-71.

Ducatel, K. and Miles, I. (1991) *Organisational Modernisation: The Human Dimension of Technology Change,* Report to EC/DGV (mimeo), Manchester: PREST, University of Manchester.

Earl, E. (1989) *Management Strategies for Information Technology.* Englewood Cliffs, NJ: Prentice Hall.

Freeman, C. (1994) Critical survey: the economics of technical change. *Cambridge Journal of Economics,* 18, 463-514.

Freeman, C. and Perez, C. (1988) Structural crisis of adjustment, business cycles and investment behaviour. In *Technical Change and Economic Theory*, ed. G. Dosi *et al*., 38–66. London: Pinter.

Gallouj, F. (forthcoming) Neo-Schumpeterian perspectives on innovation in services. In *Services and Innovation in the Knowledge Economy*, ed. I. Miles and M. Boden. London: Continuum 488.

Grönroos, C. (1978) A service-oriented approach to marketing of services. *European Journal of Marketing*, 12(8), 589.

Hauknes, J. (1996) *Innovation in the Service Economy*. Oslo, Norway, STEP report (available at http:\\www.step.no\).

Holmlund, M. and Kock, S. (1996) Relationship marketing—The importance of customer perceived service quality in retail. *Service Industries Journal*, 16(3), 287-304.

Howells, J. and Green, A. (1988) *Technological Innovation, Structural Change and Location in UK Services*. Aldershot: Avebury.

Howells, J. and Hine, J. (1991) Competitive strategy and the implementation of a new network technologies: the case of EFTPOS in the UK. *Technology Analysis and Strategic Management*, 3(4), 397-425

Hoy, E.W., Wicks, E.K. and Forland, R.A. (1996) A guide to facilitating consumer choice. *Health Affairs*, 15(4), 9-30.

Ingham, H. and Thompson, S. (1993) The adoption of new technology in financial services: The case of building societies. *Economic Innovation and New Technology*, 2, 263-74.

Kay, J. (1993) *Foundations of Corporate Success*. Oxford: Oxford University Press.

Kotler, P. (1980) *Principles of Marketing*. Englewood Cliffs, NJ: Prentice-Hall.

Kotler, P. (1994) *Marketing Management: Analysis, Planning, Implementation and Control*, 9th edn. New Jersey: Prince Hall, Inc.

Lawes, A. (1993) The benefits of quality management to the library and information services profession. *Special Libraries*, 84(3), 142-46.

Martin, L.L. (1993) Total quality management—The new managerial wave. *Administration in Social Work*, 17(2), 1-16.

Miles, I. (1987) Information technology and the services economy. *Oxford Surveys in Information Technology*, 4, 25-56.

———, (1993) Services in the new industrial economy. *Futures*, July/August, 653-72.

———, (1994) Innovation in services. In *The Handbook of Industrial Innovation*, ed. M. Dodgson and R. Rothwell, p. 243.

Cheltnham, Edward Elgar (1996) *Innovation in Services: Services in Innovation*. Manchester: Manchester Statistical Society.

Miller, D. and Friesen, P.H. (1986) Porters (1980) Generic strategies and performance: an empirical examination with American data—Part I: Testing Porter. *Organisation Studies*, 7(1), 37-55.

Murray, F. (1989) The organisational politics of information technology: studies from the UK financial services industry. *Technology Analysis and Strategic Management*, 1(30), 285-97.

Nelson, R.R. (1991) Why do firms differ, and how does it matter? *Strategic Management Journal*, 12, 61-74.

Nelson, R.R. and Winter, S.G. (1977) In search of useful theory of innovation. *Research Policy*, 6, 36-76, *Competition and IT-based Innovation in Banking Services*, 489.

Pennings, J.M. and Harianton, F. (1992) The diffusion of technological innovation in the commercial banking industry. *Strategic Management Journal*, 13, 29-46.

Pettigrew, A. (1985) *The Awakening Giant: Continuity and Change at ICI*. Oxford: Blackwell.

Philip, G. *et al.* (1995) Technology management and information technology strategy: preliminary results of an empirical study of Canadian organisations. *International Journal of Information Management*, 15(4), 303-15.

Porter, M.E. (1980) *The Competitive Strategies: Techniques for Analysing Industries and Competition*. New York: Free Press.

———, (1985) *Competitive Advantage: Creating and Sustaining Superior Performance*. Free Press: New York.

———, (1990) *Competitive Advantages of Nations*. London: Macmillan

Quinn, J. and Paqutte, P. (1990b) Technology in services: creating organisation revolutions. *Sloan Management Review*, Winter: 67-77.

Rogers, E.M. (1993) *Diffusion of Innovation*. New York: Free Press.

Rothwell, R. (1986) Innovation and re-innovation: a role for the user. *Journal of Marketing Management*, 2(2), 109-23.

Schroeder, D.M. (1990) A dynamic perspective on the impact of process innovation upon competitive strategies. *Strategic Management Journal*, 11, 25-41.

Thomas, G. and Miles, I. (1989) *Telematics in Transition: The Development of New Interactive Service in the United Kingdom*. Essex: Longman.

Utterback, J.M. (1979) Product and process innovation in a changing competitive environment. In *Industrial Innovation: Technology, Policy, Diffusion*, ed. M.J. Baker, pp. 135-47. London: Macmillan.

———, (1994) *Mastering the Dynamics of Innovation: How Companies Can Seize Opportunities in the Face of Technological Change*. Boston, Mass.: Harvard Business School Press.

Utterback, J. and Abernathy, W.J. (1975) A dynamic model of process and product innovation. *International Journal of Management Science*, 3(6), 424-41.

Vernon, R. (1966) International investment and international trade in the product cycle. *Quarterly Journal of Economics*, 80, 190-207.

www.infogile.com

# A Study on Non-Performing Assets (NPAs) in Indian Scheduled Commercial Banks

N. SUNDARAM AND C.M. MARAN

## INTRODUCTION

The concept of 'non-recognition of income' on bad and doubtful debts assets is not new to the Indian Banking System. This practice was in vogue since a very long time, much before "Introduction of prudential norms" on Income recognition and Asset classification. But what was not defined in certain terms, as to when these were to be classified 'Loan Past Due' or 'Non-Performing', so as not to recognize the income. Further the procedure prevailing in bank was to recognize the income on accrual basis through quality of asset (loan) was not good. This facilitated the banks to present a rosy Balance sheet, higher than a true one, which lead to wide criticism by public and press.

After failure of several International Banks, the Bank for International settlement appointed a committee (known as Basle Committee) to look in to the adequacy of capital of banks with international presence. The Basle Committee on banking supervision comprised representatives of the central bank and supervisory authority of group 10 of countries (Belgium, Canada, France, Germany, Italy, Japan, Netherlands, Sweden, UK and USA). The report submitted by the Committee in July 1988 contains a detailed framework of recommendations agreed between all group 10 countries for measurement of capital adequacy and establishment of minimum standards, to be achieved by the end of 1992, for Banks operating internationally.

Participating in global trades and other mercantile activities require, adhering to the international standards/ yardsticks and also rating by international agencies on the ability of the domestic financial systems, to withstand the international instability and to access to the capital markets as well. This is called for a reform in financial sector with utmost priority in a liberalizing economy.

Therefore, Central Government constituted a Committee on financial systems under the Chairmanship of Mr. M. Narasimham to examine various issues affecting financial systems and suggest measures to improve the same. The Committee submitted its recommendations in November 1991 and the RBI inter-accepted the major recommendations as regards Asset classification, income recognition for the purpose of provisioning and other related matters.

In order to bring further reforms in financial sector/ systems, the government constituted another committee in 1997 under the championship of Mr. Narasimham and it submitted its 2nd report in April 1998 covering broad inter-related issues of action that need to be taken to strengthen Banking system, streamlining procedures and structural changes in the system.

## REVIEW OF LITERATURE

The Report of the committee on banking sector reforms, 1998, (chairman: Shri. M. Narasimham) has acknowledged the importance of the fact that NPAs of large magnitudes are a major impediment to the healthy performance of the banking sector. The Committee had underlined the need to reduce the average level of net NPAs for all banks to 3 percent by 2002 and to zero for banks with interventional presence.

It is widely agreed that the built-up of Non-performing Assets has been an important factor that has eroded the profitability of public sector banks (PSBs) in India. The Gross NPAs of PSBs has removed up from Rs. 39,253 crore in 1993 to Rs. 45,653 crore in 1998. As per cent of gross advances, NPAs of PSBs stood at 16% as at end March 1998, and these were significantly higher than that of the developed economies like the USA (1.1%), Finland (2.7%), Norway (3.2%) and even the Asian economies like Malaysia (3.9%) and Japan (3.4%).

The Public Sector Banks (PSBs) had been forced by the government—in agriculture and industry to lend to dubious parties and large proportion of these loans became doubtful debts, commonly known as Non-Performing Loans. For this NPAs in Public Sector Banks (PSBs), the Government of India in general and the Finance Ministry in particular was directly or indirectly.

The recovery of NPAs got a booster after the enactment of SARFAESI Act, 2002. There was a decline in gross NPAs from Rs. 70,860 crores in 2001-02 to Rs. 64,790 crores in 2003-04.

The Indian banking sector is facing a serious problem of NPA. The extent of NPA is comparatively higher in public sector banks. To improve the efficiency and profitability, the NPA has to be reduced. Various steps have been taken by government to reduce the NPA. It is highly impossible to have zero percentage NPA. But at least Indian banks can try competing with foreign banks to maintain international standards.

There was a significant decline in the non-performing assets (NPAs) of SCBs in 2003-04, despite adoption of 90 day delinquency norm from March 31, 2004. The gross NPAs of SCBs declined from 4.0 percent of total assets in 2002-03 to 3.3 percent in 2003-04. The corresponding decline in net NPAs was from 1.9 per cent to 1.2 per cent. Both gross NPAs and net

NPAs declined in absolute terms. While the gross NPAs declined from Rs. 68,717 crore in 2002-03 to Rs. 64,787 crore in 2003-04, net NPAs declined from Rs. 32,670 crore to Rs. 24,617 crore in the same period. There was also a significant decline in the proportion of net NPAs to net advances from 4.4 per cent in 2002-03 to 2.9 per cent in 2003-04. The significant decline in the net NPAs by 24.7 per cent in 2003-04 as compared to 8.1 per cent in 2002-03 was mainly on account of higher provisions (up to 40.0 per cent) for NPAs made by SCBs.

## OBJECTIVES OF THE STUDY

The study aims to gain insights into the position of non-performing assets in commercial banking. The following broad objections are laid down for the purpose of the study.

- To study the impact of Non-Performance Assets in Indian commercial-banking industry.
- To know the position of Non-Performing Assets in commercial banks.
- To study the level of Non-Performing Assets in scheduled commercial banks.
- To look over the remedies available to reduce the Non-Performance Assets in Indian Commercial banking industry.
- To suggest ways and means to avoid the Non Performance Assets in Indian Commercial industry.

## METHODOLOGY

The study is based mainly on secondary data. The Annual Reports of the Reserve Bank of India provides the necessary data. To supplement the data, the researcher elicits other relevant information available from the records of the various Public Sector Institutions, Private Sector Institutions, Co-operative banks and Regional Rural banks. Magazines, journals, various reports on non-performance assets, websites, and text books were also referred.

## PERIOD OF STUDY

The study is confined to a period of 5 years i.e., from 2002-07.

## TOOLS OF ANALYSIS

The concerned information has been processed with the help of the computer. Statistical tools like Percentage analysis and Correlation analysis have been used to analyse the data. Graphs and diagrams were also given to give a clear picture of the position on Non-Performing Assets over the period.

## NON-PERFORMING ASSETS (NPAs)

An asset which ceases to yield income for the bank should be treated as Non-Performing Asset (NPA) and any income from such loan Asset should not be booked as income until it is actually recovered. NPA shall have well defined credit weakness which jeopardize the liquidation of the debt and are characterized by distinct possibility that the Bank would sustain some loss if the deficiencies are not corrected.

An account is to be treated as Non-Performing Asset (NPA) when it ceases to generate income for the Bank.

Non-Performing Assets (NPA) means as asset or account of borrower, which has been classified by a bank a financial institution as sub-standard, doubtful or loss asset, in accordance with the directions or guidelines relating to asset classification issued by RBI.

Non-performing assets, also called non-performing loans, are on which repayments or interest payments are not bearing made on time.

With effect from 31, 2001, a Non-performing Asset (NPA) shall be an advance where :

Interest and/or instalment of principal remain overdue for a period of more than 180 days in respect of a term loan.

The account remains 'out of order' for a period of more than 180 days, in respect of an Over draft/Cash Credit. The bill remains overdue for a period of more than 180 days in the case of bill purchased and discounted.

Interest and/or instalment of principal remains overdue for two harvest seasons but for a period not exceeding two half year in the case of an advance granted for agricultural purpose, and Any amount to be received remains overdue for a period of more than 180 days in respect of other accounts.

With a view to moving towards international best practices and to ensure greater transparency, it has been decided to adopt the '90 days overdue' norm for identification of NPAs, form the year ending March 31, 2004. Accordingly, with effect from March 31, 2004 a Non-Performing Asset (NPA) shall be a loan or an advance where:

Interest and/or instalment of principal remain overdue for a period of more than 90 days in respect of a term loan. The account remains 'out of order' for a period of more than 90 days, irrespective of an Over Draft/Cash Credit.

The bill remains overdue for a period of more than 90 days in the case of bill purchased and discounted.

Interest and/or instalment of principal remains overdue for two harvest seasons but for a period not exceeding two half year in the case of an advance granted for agricultural purpose, and any amount to be received remains overdue for a period of more than 90 days in respect of other accounts.

## NPAs IN SCHEDULED COMMERCIAL BANKS

Commercial Banks play an important role in the economic development of the country. They act as catalyst, in commercial and industrial activities. The commercial bank receives money from the depositors and lend it to trade, commerce and industry. The primary objective of any commercial bank is to earn profit.

### Structure of Commercial Banks

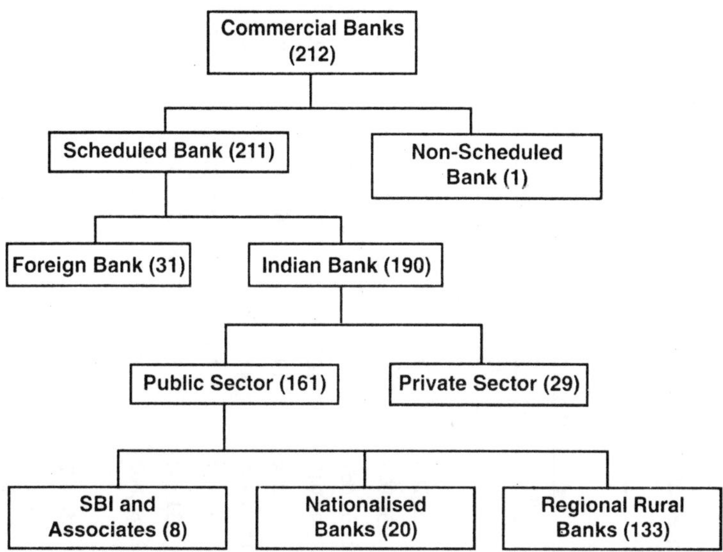


In India commercial banks are classified into schedule and non-schedule banks. At present there are 212 commercial banks in India on at March 2006.

### Sector-wise NPAs

The consolidated statement of public and private sector banks with respect to sector wise NPA indicates that the NPAs in the priority sector increased during 2006-07. This was mainly due to increase in NPAs in the agriculture sector, while NPAs in the SSI sector declined. The NPAs in the public sector also increased during the year. However, NPAs in the non-priority sector declined during 2006-07. At the aggregate level, the share of priority sector NPAs was the highest at 54.1 per cent, of which priority sector NPAs other than agriculture and SSIs constituted almost a quarter (25.1 per cent) of the total NPAs. The share of on-priority sector NPAs was 44.9 per cent during 2006-07.

TABLE I

## Consolidated Balance Sheet of Scheduled Commercial Banks

| Item | As at end-March | | | |
|---|---|---|---|---|
| | 2006 | | 2007 | |
| | Amount | Per cent to total | Amount | Per cent to total |
| (1) | (2) | (3) | (4) | (5) |
| **Liabilities** | | | | |
| 1. Capital | 25,206 | 0.9 | 29,559 | 0.9 |
| 2. Reserve and Surplus | 1,57,974 | 5.7 | 1,89,615 | 5.5 |
| 3. Deposits | 21,64,681 | 77.7 | 26,96,980 | 77.9 |
| 3.1. Demand Deposits | 2,92,945 | 10.5 | 3,51,998 | 10.2 |
| 3.2. Saving Bank Deposits | 5,42,874 | 19.5 | 6,31,651 | 18.2 |
| 3.3. Term Deposits | 13,28,861 | 47.7 | 17,13,330 | 49.5 |
| 4. Borrowings | 2,03,147 | 7.3 | 2,42,870 | 7 |
| 5. Other Liabilities and Provisions | 2,34,852 | 8.4 | 3,04,381 | 8.8 |
| Total Liabilities/Assets | 27,85,863 | 100 | 34,63,406 | 100 |
| **Assets** | | | | |
| 1. Cash and Balances with RBI | 1,44,475 | 5.2 | 1,95,372 | 5.6 |
| 2. Balances with Banks and Money at Call and Short Notice | 1,16,443 | 4.2 | 1,58,413 | 4.6 |
| 3. Investments | 8,66,508 | 31.1 | 9,50,769 | 27.5 |

| | | | | |
|---|---|---|---|---|
| 3.1. Government Securities (a+b) | 6,90,421 | 24.8 | 7,54,456 | 21.8 |
| a. In India | 6,86,464 | 24.6 | 7,50,733 | 21.7 |
| b. Outside India | 3,957 | 0.1 | 3,723 | 0.1 |
| 3.2. Other Approved Securities | 13,949 | 0.5 | 12,760 | 0.4 |
| 3.3. Non-Approved Securities | 1,62,137 | 5.8 | 1,83,551 | 5.3 |
| 4. Loans and Advances | 15,16,811 | 54.4 | 19,81,216 | 57.2 |
| 4.1. Bills Purchased and Discounted | 1,03,657 | 3.7 | 1,24,424 | 3.6 |
| 4.2. Cash Credits, Overdrafts, etc. | 5,65,001 | 20.3 | 7,12,866 | 20.6 |
| 4.3. Term Loans | 8,48,152 | 30.4 | 11,43,924 | 33 |
| 5. Fixed Assets | 25,081 | 0.9 | 31,362 | 0.9 |
| 6. Other Assets | 1,16,542 | 4.2 | 1,46,271 | 4.2 |

*Source* : Report on Trend and Progress of Banking in India, 2006-07, Reserve Bank of India.

TABLE 2

**Growth of Balance Sheet of Scheduled Commercial Banks—Bank Group-wise**

(Percent)

| Item | As at end-March | | | | | | | | | |
|---|---|---|---|---|---|---|---|---|---|---|
| | 2006 | | | | | 2007 | | | | |
| | Public Sector Banks | Old Private Sector Banks | New Private Sector Banks | Foreign Banks | All SCBs | Public Sector Banks | Old Private Sector Banks | New Private Sector Banks | Foreign Banks | All SCBs |
| (1) | (2) | (3) | (4) | (5) | (6) | (7) | (8) | (9) | (10) | (11) |
| 1. Capital | -20.6 | 25.9 | 14.2 | 27.5 | -2.7 | 0.7 | 4.4 | 5.6 | 45.4 | 17.3 |
| 2. Reserve and Surplus | 21.7 | 19.5 | 55.2 | 28.5 | 27.7 | 20.0 | 11.6 | 17.4 | 30.6 | 20.0 |
| 3. Deposits | 12.9 | 11.6 | 50.7 | 31.7 | 17.8 | 22.9 | 6.0 | 38.8 | 32.6 | 24.6 |
| 3.1. Demand Deposits | 20.8 | 15.7 | 29.3 | 48.8 | 24.9 | 19.3 | 3.9 | 36.7 | 11.8 | 20.2 |
| 3.2. Saving Bank Deposits | 19.0 | 20.4 | 60.6 | 21.1 | 22.0 | 15.0 | 6.7 | 33.3 | 16.3 | 16.4 |
| 3.3. Term Deposits | 8.9 | 8.9 | 53.9 | 25.4 | 14.7 | 27.3 | 6.1 | 40.6 | 52.3 | 28.9 |
| 4. Borrowings | 23.7 | 22.5 | 11.0 | 24.5 | 20.7 | 5.7 | 22.3 | 42.8 | 32.7 | 19.6 |
| 5. Other Liabilities and Provisions | 12.3 | 13.8 | 34.0 | 31.4 | 17.4 | 16.2 | 16.1 | 51.1 | 88.7 | 29.6 |
| Total Liabilities/Assets | 13.6 | 12.4 | 43.2 | 29.8 | 18.3 | 21.1 | 7.1 | 38.7 | 39.5 | 24.3 |

| Assets | | | | | | | | | | |
|---|---|---|---|---|---|---|---|---|---|---|
| 1. Cash and Balances with RBI | 25.3 | -0.3 | 16.1 | 20.0 | 22.4 | 26.1 | 25.9 | 94.3 | 49.8 | 35.2 |
| 2. Balances with Banks and Money at Call and Short Notice | 14.0 | 7.5 | 37.4 | 64.3 | 22.1 | 26.9 | 5.8 | 91.9 | 42.2 | 36.0 |
| 3. Investments | -7.7 | 1.1 | 71.1 | 22.2 | -0.4 | 4.9 | -3.6 | 26.4 | 36.4 | 9.7 |
| 3.1. Government Securities (a+b) | -8.4 | 3.2 | 50.4 | 20.1 | -1.2 | 3.6 | -2.2 | 33.0 | 37.5 | 9.3 |
| a. In India | -8.5 | 3.2 | 50.3 | 20.1 | -1.3 | 3.6 | -2.0 | 32.9 | 37.5 | 9.4 |
| b. Outside India | 15.3 | 2.6 | 255.2 | — | 17.7 | -8.6 | -100.0 | 125.0 | — | -5.9 |
| 3.2. Other Approved Securities | -13.5 | -14.4 | -60.9 | -60.6 | -14.4 | -7.8 | -30.9 | -20.7 | 0.2 | -8.5 |
| 3.3. Non-Approved Securities | -2.8 | -5.8 | 24.1 | 32.8 | 4.8 | 13.6 | -7.6 | 11.4 | 32.7 | 13.2 |
| 4. Loans and Advances | 29.5 | 21.7 | 50.2 | 29.5 | 31.8 | 30.2 | 12.0 | 39.9 | 29.5 | 30. |
| 4.1. Bills Purchased and Discounted | 16.5 | 8.1 | -10.4 | 27.0 | 12.8 | 22.4 | -15.4 | 21.8 | 21.3 | 20.0 |
| 4.2. Cash Credits, Overdrafts, etc. | 26.9 | 21.4 | 64.2 | 33.7 | 29.3 | 25.7 | 11.6 | 42.0 | 27.7 | 26.2 |
| 4.3. Term Loans | 33.5 | 24.3 | 54.4 | 26.6 | 36.4 | 34.5 | 16.5 | 40.7 | 32.8 | 34.9 |
| 5. Fixed Assets | 9.1 | 7.4 | 2.5 | 28.1 | 8.8 | 37.7 | -5.6 | 4.2 | 24.4 | 25.0 |
| 6. Other Assets | 12.8 | 14.3 | 31.3 | 30.7 | 18.4 | 7.1 | 0.7 | 33.3 | 90.6 | 25.5 |

*Source* : Report on Trend and Progress of Banking in India, 2006-07, Reserve Bank of India.

### Table 3
## Gross NPAs of Scheduled Commercial Banks— Bank Group-wise

*(As at end-March) (Amount in Rs. Crore)*

| *Bank Group* | *Year* | *Gross Advances* | *Gross NPAs* | *% to Gross Advances* | *% to Total Assets* |
|---|---|---|---|---|---|
| Public Sector Banks | 2002-03 | 5,77,813 | 54,090 | 9.4 | 4.2 |
| | 2003-04 | 6,61,975 | 51,537 | 7.8 | 3.5 |
| | 2004-05 | 8,77,825 | 48,399 | 5.5 | 2.7 |
| | 2005-06 | 11,34,724 | 41,358 | 3.6 | 2.1 |
| | 2006-07 | 14,64,493 | 38,968 | 2.7 | 1.6 |
| Old Private Sector Banks | 2002-03 | 51,329 | 4,550 | 8.9 | 4.3 |
| | 2003-04 | 57,908 | 4,398 | 7.6 | 3.6 |
| | 2004-05 | 70,412 | 4,200 | 6.0 | 3.1 |
| | 2005-06 | 85,154 | 3,759 | 4.4 | 2.5 |
| | 2006-07 | 94,872 | 2,969 | 3.1 | 1.8 |
| New Private Sector Banks | 2002-03 | 94,718 | 7,232 | 7.6 | 3.8 |
| | 2003-04 | 1,19,511 | 5,983 | 5.0 | 2.4 |
| | 2004-05 | 1,27,420 | 4,582 | 3.6 | 1.6 |
| | 2005-06 | 2,32,536 | 4,052 | 1.7 | 1.0 |
| | 2006-07 | 3,25,273 | 6,287 | 1.9 | 1.1 |
| Foreign Banks | 2002-03 | 54,184 | 2,845 | 5.3 | 2.4 |
| | 2003-04 | 62,632 | 2,894 | 4.6 | 2.1 |
| | 2004-05 | 77,026 | 2,192 | 2.8 | 1.4 |
| | 2005-06 | 98,965 | 1,928 | 1.9 | 1.0 |
| | 2006-07 | 1,27,872 | 2,263 | 1.8 | 0.8 |
| Scheduled Commercial Banks | 2002-03 | 7,78,043 | 68,717 | 8.80 | 4.00 |
| | 2003-04 | 9,02,026 | 64,812 | 7.2 | 3.3 |
| | 2004-05 | 11,52,682 | 59,373 | 5.2 | 2.5 |
| | 2005-06 | 15,51,378 | 51,097 | 3.3 | 1.8 |
| | 2006-07 | 20,12,510 | 50,486 | 2.5 | 2.5 |

*Source* : Report on Trend and Progress of Banking in India, Reserve Bank of India.

**Pearson's Correlation**

There is no significant relationship between Gross Advances and Gross NPAs of Scheduled Commercial Banks.

**Correlation between Gross Advances and Gross NPAs of Scheduled Commercial Banks**

| | | *Gross Advances* | *Gross NPAs* |
|---|---|---|---|
| Gross Advances | Pearson Correlation | 1.000 | -0.952 |
| Gross NPAs | Pearson Correlation | -0.952 | 1.000 |

*Result* : There is a high negative correlation between Gross Advances and Gross NPAs.

**Gross NPAs of Scheduled Commercial Banks**

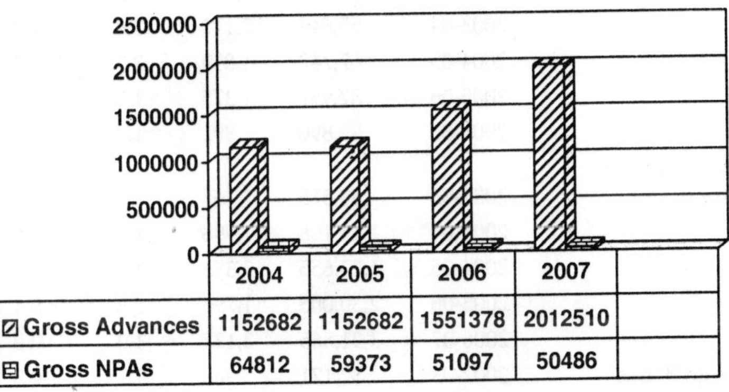


**Net NPAs of Scheduled Commercial Banks**

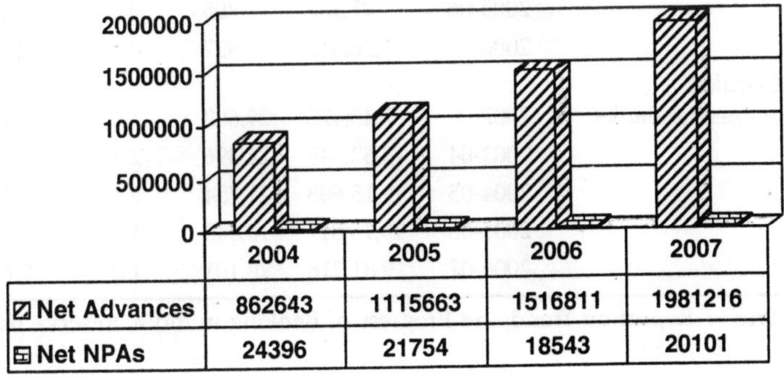

Table 4

**Net NPAs of Scheduled Commercial Banks—Bank Group-wise**

*(As at end-March) (Amount in Rs. crore)*

| *Bank Group* | *Year* | *Net Advances* | *Net NPAs* | *% to Net Advances* | *% to Total Assets* |
|---|---|---|---|---|---|
| Public Sector Banks | 2002-03 | 5,49,351 | 24,877 | 4.5 | 1.9 |
| | 2003-04 | 6,31,383 | 19,335 | 3.1 | 1.3 |
| | 2004-05 | 8,48,912 | 16,904 | 2.1 | 1.0 |
| | 2005-06 | 11,06,288 | 14,566 | 1.3 | 0.7 |
| | 2006-07 | 14,40,123 | 15,145 | 1.1 | 0.6 |
| Old Private Sector Banks | 2002-03 | 49,436 | 25,148 | 5.2 | 2.5 |
| | 2003-04 | 55,648 | 2,142 | 3.8 | 1.8 |
| | 2004-05 | 67,742 | 1,859 | 2.7 | 1.4 |
| | 2005-06 | 82,957 | 1,375 | 1.7 | 0.9 |
| | 2006-07 | 92,890 | 891 | 1.0 | 0.6 |
| New Private Sector Banks | 2002-03 | 89,515 | 1,365 | 1.5 | 0.7 |
| | 2003-04 | 1,15,106 | 1,986 | 1.7 | 0.8 |
| | 2004-05 | 1,23,655 | 2,353 | 1.9 | 0.8 |
| | 2005-06 | 2,30,005 | 1,796 | 0.8 | 0.4 |
| | 2006-07 | 3,21,865 | 3,137 | 1.0 | 0.5 |
| Foreign Banks | 2002-03 | 52,171 | 903 | 1.7 | 0.8 |
| | 2003-04 | 60,506 | 933 | 1.5 | 0.7 |
| | 2004-05 | 75,354 | 639 | 0.8 | 0.4 |
| | 2005-06 | 97,562 | 808 | 0.8 | 0.4 |
| | 2006-07 | 1,26,339 | 927 | 0.7 | 0.3 |
| Scheduled Commercial Banks | 2002-03 | 7,40,473 | 29,692 | 4.0 | 1.8 |
| | 2003-04 | 8,62,643 | 24,396 | 2.8 | 1.2 |
| | 2004-05 | 11,15,663 | 21,754 | 2.0 | 0.9 |
| | 2005-06 | 15,16,811 | 18,543 | 1.2 | 0.7 |
| | 2006-07 | 19,81,216 | 20,101 | 1.0 | 0.6 |

*Source* : Report on Trend and Progress of Banking in India, Reserve Bank of India.

**Pearson's Correlation**

There is no significant relationship between Net Advances and Net NPAs of Scheduled Commercial Banks.

**Correlation between Net Advances and Net NPAs of Scheduled Commercial Banks**

| | | *Net Advances* | *Net NPAs* |
|---|---|---|---|
| Net Advances | Pearson Correlation | 1.000 | -0.801 |
| Net NPAs | Pearson Correlation | -0.801 | 1.000 |

*Result* : There is a high negative correlation between Net Advances and Net NPAs.

**Non-Performing Assets as Percentage of Total Assets (Scheduled Commercial Banks)**

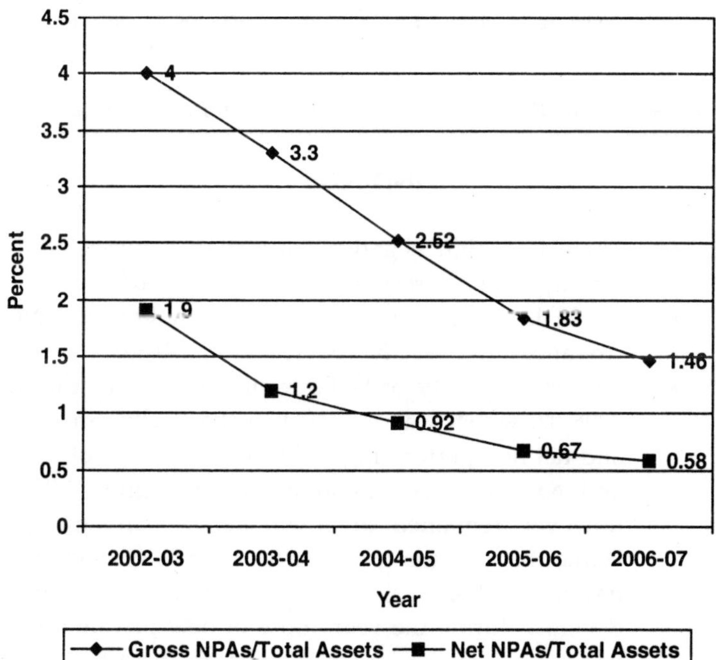

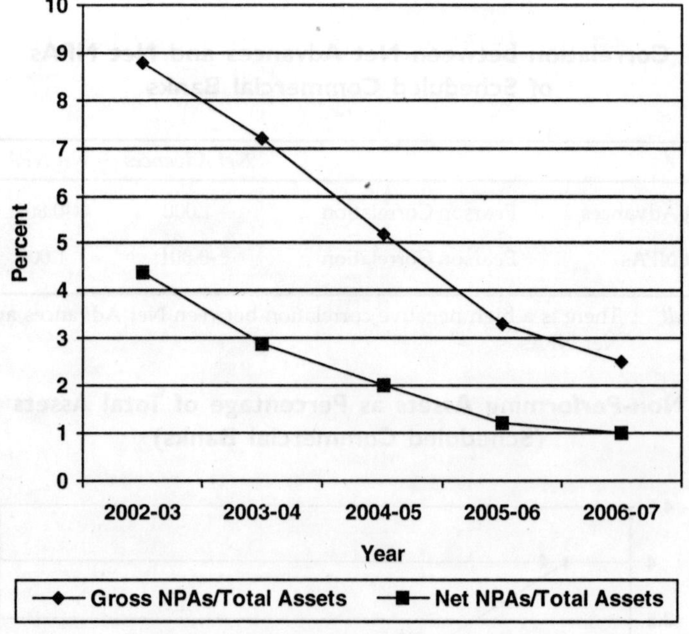


## FINDINGS

- There is a high negative correlation between Gross Advances and Gross NPAs. Therefore, -0.952.
- There is a high negative correlation between Net Advances and Net NPAs. Therefore, -0.801.
- The asset quality of SCBs improved further during 2006-07, which was reflected in the decline in gross and net non-performing assets as percentage of loans and advances. The trend in absolute gross NPAs, however, remained divergent across bank groups. While the absolute gross NPAs of PSBs (particularly, nationalized banks) and old private sector banks declined during the year, those of new private sector banks and foreign banks showed an increase.

- Non-Performing Assets (as percentage of advances).

Gross NPAs as on 2005-06 was 3.1 percentage, in 2006-07 it has decreased to 2.4 percentages.

Net NPAs as on 2005-06 was 1.2 percentage, in 2006-07 it has decreased to 1.0 percentage.

## SUGGESTIONS

- There is a need for sensitiveness and concern towards overdue position of the branch in the minds of the branch personnel.
- Change of attitude regarding the loans granted by the earlier incumbents and also under various government sponsored schemes will help achieve target-oriented and time bound programmes can only give positive results.
- Action plan and commitment on the part of branch officials to achieve target-oriented and time bound programmes can only give positive results.
- Post-sanction follow up and inspection of securities even in respect of overdue/recalled advance should be continued for effective control on security.
- Strict compliance of stipulated terms and conditions while making available the limits should be ensured. (any deviations, intentional or otherwise may affect recovery prospects at a later stage).
- Ensure correct documentation.
- Ensuring the proper end use of the loan amount.

## CONCLUSION

The Indian banking sector is facing a serious problem of NPAs. The extent of NPAs is comparatively higher in public sectors banks. To improve the efficiency and profitability, the NPAs has to be scheduled. Various steps have been taken by government to reduce the NPAs. It is highly impossible to have zero percentage NPAs. But at least Indian banks can try competing with foreign banks to maintain a international standard.

## REFERENCE

*Source* : Report of Trend and Progress of Banking in India, Reserve Bank of India, 2006-07.

### Paper

Programme on NPA and Recovery Management, Mr. Krishnamurthy, Canara Bank.

### Websites

www.Google.com
www.answers.com
www.rbi.org.in
www.wss.rbi.org.in
www.bulletin.rbi.org.in
www.AnnualReport.rbi.org.in
www.BankReport.rbi.org.in
www.nsdp.rbi.org
www.iib-online.org

# Globalization and Unmarked Inclination in Banking Sector

VIJAY PITHADIA

## INTRODUCTION

The banking sector is in a transitional mode towards a vibrant global market and sophisticated information technology. Due to this changing scenario, banks are paying more attention to expanding their activities from just lending and borrowing to other ends like, insurance merchant banking, leasing, electronic banking, etc. Even though these changes were expected after the nationalization of banks in 1969, it was noticed that it had only slow and steady progress necessitating a total revamping of the banking sector. Various reform measures were taken to strengthen the foundation of the system by improving asset quality, enhancing capital and improving profitability along with structural changes in the system. During this transition, banks have seen fierce competition, risk, and revolutionary changes forcing them to take immediate steps to retain market share, redress the grievances of customers as fast as possible by maintaining good ambience, rendering courteous services to customers with the help of latest technological innovations and products.

Globalization and liberalization have forced the banks to think in terms of technology benefits and quality service to customers as future is full of challenges and survival will be a difficult task. The entry of IT infrastructure in the corporate world of banks has brought with it many innovations, in particular the Internet. Though these changes had started with Narasimham Committee's (1992) suggestions for computerization and were followed by Saraf Committee's (1994) recommendations for electronic fund transfers (EFT), Electronic Clearing Services (ECS) and automatic data capture, the banks were actually required to use the BANKET and RBINET and Internet to accommodate itself to the innumerous transactions that had resulted as a result of globalization and liberalization.

The Indian banking industry is not lagging behind; it has started providing services electronically over the internet. These services rendered over electronic media include:

- Phone banking
- ATM—Automatic Teller Machines
- Credit Cards
- Electronic Fund Transfer—EFT
- Shared Payment Network System—SPNS
- Electronic Clearing Service—ECS
- Point of Sale—POS
- D-Mat Accounts
- Electronic Data Interchange
- E-Cheque
- Corporate Banking Terminal

## INFORMATION TECHNOLOGY

The term "information technology" describes the phenomenon created by the convergence of technologies associated with computing, communication and office systems. In the past, most accounting procedures in banks were paper-oriented. With the advent of new techniques like computers, electronic equipments and communication network, the modern accounting system have undergone a sea-change both in their preparation and presentation. The traditional system of preparing the account at quarterly, half yearly and annual lost their relevance since the information are constantly up-dated and made available at any time and anywhere. The information technology enabled the banking organizations to redesign and restructure their functioning.

These services provided by using electronic technology and media are called information technology or electronic banking or e-banking. E-banking has given an opportunity for banks to find solutions to management problems like saving time money and energy or customers by reducing/minimizing paper works, waiting in queues, lack of communication and lack of efficiency. E-banking has provided ease and flexibility in banking operations. The recommendations of Narasimham Committee (1998), for the free and liberal entry of foreign banks in India have further improved the scope for e-banking. As many foreign banks and private sector banks like CITI Bank and ICICI, HDFC banks brought with them IT-based products like ATM, credit cards, debit cards, on-line banking-etc. This forced the public sector banks and other banks to think on the same lines as these services would help banks to retain their customers, target on banking products and services more effectively to customers. Customers are also benefited as they are given more free time to indulge in e-commerce business. Therefore, after 1980 throughout the world with majority of banking transactions done through nets or by using information technology. So the information technology solves many problems of the banking industry and very useful to the customers too.

## APPLICATION OF INFORMATION TECHNOLOGY

### Phone Banking

Bank on phone, provides easy access for customers to have large businesses through telephones. Data are exchanged over the phone regarding any queries, to issue instructions on balance transfer, statement of account, cheque-book, stop payments, new schemes, interest rates, etc. at any convenient time and place. Tele banking has gone a long way in providing maximum customer satisfaction within the limited infrastructure.

### Automatic Teller Machine (ATM)

Banks in the cities to provide cash dispensation to their customers around the clock install ATMs. Now, the banks provide this facility in a more sophisticated way that a customer of one bank and branch can withdraw from any other banks, at any other branch, nation-wide. In developed countries, this service is provided to their blue chip client globally. This is possible only through world-wide networking and communication system.

### Credit Cards

These plastic cards enable customers to spend whenever he/she wants within the prescribed limits and pay later. Debit card is a prepaid card with stored value, whereas credit card is post-paid with fixed limits. It is seen that spending is higher through debit cards than with credit cards, currently CITY Bank and time bank have started with Debit cards and now other banks are also following these to launch their own cards.

### Electronic Funds Transfer (EFT)

Electronic funds transfer is a system of processing and communication of payment through electronic methods. EFT assumes greater significance in the banking system as the RBI also encourages the commercial banks to adopt this technique. Inter and intra-bank transfers of funds are now made through this EFT mechanism. Transactions of high value i.e., at least more than one lakh is now made through this cost effective and quick system of settlement. Normally, payments are made through cash, cheque, drafts and credit cards. The latest in this process are the debit card system, charge, digital cash, and electronic purse and so on.

### SPNS—(Shared Payment Network System)

SPNS installed by the IBA in the city of Mumbai, enables electronic banking service like cash transactions, extended hours of banking, utility payments, cheque, point of sale facilities by the SPNS can go to any ATM linked to SPNS.

### Electronic Clearing Services [ECS]

Electronic clearing of funds from one centre to another for handling bulk transactions like salary, interest, dividend, commission etc., has dispensed the cheque. A part of electronic clearing service is computerized clearing of cheque at metropolitan centers and linking with international communication system of SWIFT. These services have contributed in a great way towards improving the customer's services globally.

### Point of Sale [POS] Terminal

Payment card at a retail location for electronic transfer of fund is called POS. The client enters his personal identification number [PIN] and confirms the amount due. Customer's account is automatically debited with the amount of purchases and it credits the retailers account POS installed at petrol stations and large retail houses are linked to banks network.

### D-Mat Accounts

Transacting shares business through electronic media is called D-Mat. Investor opens an account called Demat Accounts with DPS. They get shares in electronic form. Then they send the actual shares to the investor. Investor pays for the opening, maintenance and collection of shares. This has reduced the paper work, bad deliveries; loss of shares and less transaction cost. However delays in demating, higher cost charged by the investors has not given a good start for the growth and scope of Demat in India.

### Electronic Data Interchange—EDI

EDI refers to the electronic exchange of structure information using telecommunication like payment orders, debits credits, statement of account, etc. As part of EDI, satellite communication network is also entering the banks. EDI will very soon do away with branch banking and the customers will be identified as ban customer and not branch customer.

### E-cheque

Digital cheques used by the payer to the payee through internet are called e-cheque. Electronic versions of cheque are issued, received and processed. Most of the banks use e-cheque. A secure means of operation is provided for collecting, payments, and transferring cash flows through this method. The payer issues a digital cheque to the payee and the entire transactions are done through internet

### Computerized Accounting

Development in computer has brought about a change in the accounting practices in banks. A wide range of software packages were developed recently, which attributed to the widespread use of computers to increase the information needs. Microcomputer are used to keep records and for processing. Microcomputer is small unit capable of doing calculations, storing data and programmers. This computer range from small personal computer (PCs) to a blue chip "desk top" business computer the microcomputers are used for word processing, spreadsheet application, etc. If the computer is not properly used, and it will result in unfair accounting and loss of information.

Data base with different technology such as lost terminal, file server and client server system established all over the world. For creation, manipulation and share information, tools such as Microsoft windows were developed and applied. This Microsoft windows provide graphical user interface, window-based word processing along with window-based spreadsheet and E-mail package. Information technology now uses geographic information system (GIS) and global positioning system (GPS). GIS means type in a map to any other type of data. GIS is capable of converting data into pictures and graphs. GPS means the system, which enabled the precise navigation and targeting of many of the weapons used during the gulf war.

### E-Mail

The system of sending messages from one computer to another is known as E-mail. E-mail originally was introduced in the year 1983 in U.S.A. to send the messages through

E-mail, a mini personal computer, one telephone line, a modern and software support is required. Modern is of various types like kotex, robotex, multi-moderna, etc. The change for sending a message with 250 characters (bits) through E-mail is Rs. 2. for express it is Rs. 4. For foreign countries it is Rs. 15 per page. If it is sent through telex or fax it costs Rs. 5 extra for transmission even within our country.

There are different commands like read mail, prepare mail, mail list, status, message forward, etc. Each of these commands do different functions for example, read mail enables us to read the message sent by other to our computer.

### RBI Net : (RBI NET)

This scheme facilitates the transfer of funds by a customer former any bank, any branch, any center to his client at some other center, so other bank and/or branch. Settlements between banks and with the RBI are now a day done through this system. Inter and Intra-bank clearing are also done through this electronic communication system.

### Internet

Internet is a system interconnected with network worldwide. The increasing popularity of the Internet is the worldwide web (WWW), which connects millions of servers. In India there are 500 Internet hosts and more than 750 web sites that provide this Internet service. The Internet has 25 million computer buffs and their population explodes at a rate of 10% per month. Internet has found a nest off 150 countries. Arpanet developed by the USA in 1969 was the base for this magical development of Internet. Only those who master the computer commands can work successfully on the Internet.

The Internet has many features. E-mail is one of the simplest facilities available on the Internet. Through this Internet, a subscriber can set-up a newsletter, or a discussion through which the participants exchange their views. In the modern age, it is possible to transmit texts; pictures and voices information from anywhere, in any form in the world is accessible to the subscriber at the press of a button and at a very minimum cost. Computer on the Internet communicate with each other in a number of ways. These methods are called services. The most popular services are:

(1) Worldwide web
(2) E-mail
(3) FTP (file transfer protocol)
(4) Use net news
(5) ERNET
(6) Browser
(7) Graphic Viewers
(8) New Reader
(9) Uniform Resource Locator (URL)
(10) Hypertext Transfer Protocol (http)
(11) Gopher News
(12) Wide Area Information Service (WAIS)
(13) Application of information Technology in the Banking System

The following are the specific Areas where information technology can be used in the banking system:

(i) Preparation and posting in ledger (LAN)
(ii) Portfolio management (genetic algorithm)
(iii) Funds management and transfer (on-line banking)
(iv) Credit appraisal
(v) Foreign exchange transaction
(vi) Opening of letter of credit
(vii) Issue of letter of guarantee
(viii) Decision-making at senior manager level
(ix) Employees training and education
(x) Preparation and submission of financial statements
(xi) Identification of fraudulent credit card transactions (neutral network system)

**Benefits**

The information technology can be administered in the banking system. The application of information technology will help in increasing the operating efficiency of the banking system. Its application will result in saving in cost. The quality of the information can be improved. The branches can provide improved customer services. This will enable the domestic banks to face and challenge the competition from their foreign rivals. There will be a reduction in the staff strength to a considerable extent due to the adoption of information technology. The working condition of the bank branches can be improved.

## Benefits of E-Banking Services

- It reduces cost of both in services and administration
- Overcoming the geographical barriers
- Cost minimized for customers
- It helps to maintain customer loyalty
- Web site enable banks to develop advertisement
- Information technology enable banks to deliver products and services
- Multimedia capabilities offer homogenous branding
- Online banking encourages promotion of various schemes of the bank
- Individualized and customized services with the help of integrated customer data
- Minimizing fraud and misappropriation by inter-branch reconciliation
- Convenience to customers—like card free banking, cash free banking provides a domain of access to banking services.

## Reasons for Poor Achievement

(1) Poor initial introduction of the information technology concepts in the banks

(2) Improper implementation of techniques of information technology

(3) Improper selection of hardware and software result in heavy cost and inefficiency

(4) Inadequate suppliers support after the purchase of the IT system

(5) Fear and reluctance among the staff regarding reduction of staff followed by retrenchment due to the introduction of information technology

(6) Brain drain is yet another cause for the poor implementation of the information technology

(7) Lack of co-ordination between the management and staff is another reason for the poor achievement.

## CONCLUSION

The current trends are quite comforting for customer—but it does pose threats and problems to banks. As we find information technology invading the banking sector, only banks, which used the right technology, could come out with success. Banks are required to 'restructure', re-invent and reengineer themselves go meet the necessary performance improvement and get the competitive edge due to the introduction of information technology (e-banking) being an important output of ;information technology has ushered in an era which is transforming the entire functioning of banks. The tilt in the banks from traditional to modern e-banking services has been welcomed due its advantages, but banks in India are taking time to get rooted. Banks are slow but are going to offer in further more e-banking services to keep in pace with the evolving pattern of customers' demand.

The flexibility of e-banking offers unprecedented opportunities for the bank to reach out to its customers. With the rapid expansion of the Internet facilities, e-banking is all set to play a very important role in the 21st century. Banks have to deal with the sophisticated clientele with the help of latest technology like e-banking. E-banking if taken in the right way by banks and customers would take the economy to its best and make it a boon to customers

## REFERENCES

G.S. Mongia, R.K. Sinha, Nationalization of Banks : Retrospect and Prospects, R.V. Kulkarni, B.L. Desai, Knowledge-based system on Banking Sector.

I.V. Trivedi, Indian Banking in the new millennium.

M.P. Jaiswal, Anjali Kaushik, e-CRM-Business System Frontiers.

Dr. C.S. Rayudu, E-Commerce, E-Business.

E-Commercem, S. Pankaj.

Developing Accounting: Point Publishers, Jaipur 2005, pp. 489-93.

*Journal of Accounting and Finance,* Vol. vii, No. 1 Spring 2004, pp. 14-24.

*Journal of Accounting and Finance,* Vol. ix, No. 1 Spring 2004, pp. 76-89.

Banking Finance, Vol. vii, No. 7, July 2005, pp. 3-4.

*Indian Overseas Bank, Quarterly News Review,* Vol. vii, No. 1, Jan.-March 2004, pp. 10-12.

*Punjab National Bank Monthly Review,* July, 2003, pp. 346-53.

*The Week,* 17 Sep. 2003, pp. 28-29.

*The Banker,* Sep. 2004, p. 20.

*Information Communication World,* Oct. 2005, pp. 11-14.

*SBI Monthly Review,* Oct. 2003, pp. 521-27.

# 6

# *Customer Relationship Management Related to Banking Sector*

N. SUMATHI AND J. JAYASHREE

## ABSTRACT

"CRM is a business strategy to select and manage the most valuable customer relationships. CRM requires a customer-centric business philosophy and culture to support effective marketing, sales, and service processes. CRM applications can enable effective customer relationship management, provided that an enterprise has the right leadership, strategy, and culture." Customer Relationship Management is a customer-focused business strategy designed to optimize revenue, profitability, and customer loyalty.

Bank customers are frequently segmented into groups based on the number of products used and balances held. Large group of customers most often approach the bank through branches or call centres. Bank customers are serviced through four main channels, these are ATMs, Bank tellers, Banking consultants, the contact centre. Meeting the rapidly changing needs of customers is at the heart of a successful banking enterprise. CRM is a sound business strategy to identify the bank's most profitable customers and prospects, and devotes time and attention to expanding account relationships with those customers through individualized marketing, repricing, discretionary decision-making, and customized service—all delivered through the various sales channels that the bank uses. Regulation and technological improvements are responsible for the vast majority of innovations in banking over the past quarter century. The latest trend in banking strategy is clicks and bricks in which customer can debit or credit accounts, check balances and even trade on it. The primary business driver of message-based middleware solutions in the banking industry is Customer Relationship Management, the business of customer acquisition, customer development and customer retention.

## INTRODUCTION

"CRM is a business strategy to select and manage the most valuable customer relationships. CRM requires a customer-centric business philosophy and culture to support effective marketing, sales, and service processes. CRM applications can enable effective customer relationship management, provided that an enterprise has the right leadership, strategy, and culture." (CRMguru.com, 2001).

Customer Relationship Management is a customer-focused business strategy designed to optimize revenue, profitability, and customer loyalty. By implementing a CRM strategy, an organization can improve the business processes and technology solutions around selling, marketing and servicing functions across all customer touch-points (for example: Web, e-mail, phone, fax, in-person). Financial institutions are increasingly using customer management solutions with sophisticated front-office analytics capabilities that allow them to better slice and dice their customer data and use this insight to segment their clientele for better-targeted selling opportunities. Commercial banks need to employ a customer management solution that consolidates information from all customer interactions, whether they are in-person meetings with advisors or inquiries to the call center or the Internet. Moving forward, it will be imperative that every banking representative has the ability to access a 360-degree view of any customer in real time to enhance customer retention and competitive advantage. However, the new millennium has resulted in banks and financial agencies rethinking their strategies and goals. They have come to understand the importance of hanging onto the customer and keeping him happy. The rules that once governed the banking industry have changed. They have realized that adopting a customer centric strategy is essential and needs to be compulsorily undertaken. The vast majority of banks now realize they need a customer strategy and are opting for CRM—Customer Relationship Management.

## CRM STRATEGY IN BANKING

Bank customers are frequently segmented into groups based on the number of products used and balances held. Customers with a low number of products and low balances may be treated as if they had what Day (2000) terms a 'transactional exchange relationship'. Here the focus is on providing cost effective services. Customers holding many products and high potential balances may fall into the 'value-adding' or 'collaborative' relationship categories. Transactional exchange relationships may be transformed into value adding relationships when customers take up staff recommendations for additional products such as investment or higher interest savings accounts perhaps with automatic funds transfer to optimize interest. From the bank's perspective, the account becomes value adding because the number of products and services used by the customer increases and fees earned by the Bank also increase. In addition, the increased portfolio of products decreases the probability of the customer defecting to other competitors. These clients share their financial information and plans with the bank and the bank provides financial solutions tailored specifically for them including solutions to meet seasonal cash flow fluctuations and hedging of interest or foreign exchange rates. Specialist managers with specific industry knowledge and good interpersonal skills maintain close relationships with these clients; they visit clients on their premises to strengthen the relationship and to gather information to assist the bank in developing better solutions by better anticipating client's future requirements. However, the majority of the banks' customers are transactional exchange or value-adding relationships. This large group of customers most often approach the bank through branches or call centres (sometimes referred to as customer contact centres). To manage these relationships, branch and call centre staff must be armed with both bank product information and customer information.

## BANK CUSTOMERS ARE SERVICED THROUGH FOUR MAIN CHANNELS

- ATMs.
- Bank tellers.
- Banking consultants.
- The contact centre.
- The ATMs can perform quite complex transactions but customers tend to use them for simple transactions. They are used mainly for simple transactions such as cash withdrawals or deposits, balance queries, and fund transfers between personal accounts. This channel is available twenty-four hours a day, seven days a week. It benefits both customers and the bank, being a convenience to customer while reducing the workload for branches, especially for tellers and banking consultants.
- Tellers provide all the services offered by ATMs plus customer account maintenance such as change of name or addresses, set-up of automatic payment, and changes of Personal Identification Number (PIN) on credit cards and ATM access card.
- Customers seeking advice on financial products or specialised services such as loans are referred to a banking consultant. From the bank's perspective, the primary function of a banking consultant is to sell bank services and products. Banking consultants typically come to know many of their customers

well, and become proactive in suggesting financial services to meet customers' circumstances and changing needs.

- Sales and services representatives, service customer through a call centre that is available twenty-four hours a day, seven days a week. They provide most of the services a teller can provide, with the exception of deposits and withdrawals. They also provide part of what banking consultants provide, selling financial services and products, such as credit cards and overdraft facilities, but only at lower dollar values. In addition, they reply to customer e-mails.

## CRM Challenges that Face the Banking Industry Today

- Identify customers that have the most assets and would be the most profitable.
- Identify the most profitable products.
- Cross-sell and up-sell products that is most relevant to a customer's life stage and financial needs.
- Improve customer service while reducing service costs in basic areas, such as account inquiry, transfers, the trading of financial instruments, and cash management.
- Find strategies to eliminate current operational inefficiencies.
- Implement technology that leads to enhanced productivity of customers, partners, and employees.

## Growth of Customer Relationship Management

Meeting the rapidly changing needs of customers is at the heart of a successful banking enterprise. How well a bank knows its customers—and how effectively it leverages that knowledge in the face of intense competition, shrinking margins, new technologies, and increasing customer's demands can make the difference between thriving and barely holding on. Customer relationship management (CRM) systems have provided partial solutions to complex heterogeneous banking issues. At times, technology—rather than business needs has been the driver for CRM development. But CRM solutions hold great promise for banking when there is a focus on pro- viding support for key business processes.

Customer Relationship Management (CRM) is predicted in the banking sector over the next few years. Banks are aiming to increase customer profitability with any customer retention. The role of Customer Relationship Management in banking sector and the need for Customer Relationship Management to increase customer value by using some analytical methods in CRM applications. CRM is a sound business strategy to identify the bank's most profitable customers and prospects, and devotes time and attention to expanding account relationships with those customers through individualized marketing, repricing, discretionary decision-making, and customized service—all delivered through the various sales channels that the bank uses. In banking sector, relationship management could be defined as having and acting upon deeper knowledge about the customer such as how to find the customer, get to know the customer, keep in touch with the customer, ensure that the customer gets what she/he wishes from service provider, and understand when they are not satisfied and might leave the service provider and act accordingly. CRM objectives such as growth, retention and cost reduction. Increasing customers' product cross-holdings, maximizing the contribution from each customer through time and increasing efficiency are couple of those objectives. A campaign management in a bank is conducted using data mining tasks such as dependency analysis, cluster profile analysis, concept description, deviation detection, and data visualization. Crucial business decisions with this campaign are made by extracting valid, previously unknown and ultimately comprehensible and actionable knowledge from large databases. The model developed here answers what the different customer segments are, who more likely to respond to a given offer is, which customers are the bank likely to lose, which most likely to default on credit cards is, what the risk associated with this loan applicant.

## EVOLUTION OF CRM IN BANKING SECTOR

Regulation and technological improvements are responsible for the vast majority of innovations in banking over the past quarter century. The introduction of personal computers and the proliferation of ATMs in the 1970s captured bank management's attention. The regulatory changes in the 1980S fueled much of the industry's growth, then downsizing as bankers focused on amassing market presence, which resulted in significant merger activity. Recent technological improvements are at the root of bankers' focus as well as a target of their significant investment doolers today. In fact, according to recent projections, bankers and their financial service company brethren will spend almost $7 billion this year on CRM and increase that by 14 percent each year for then next several years.

Looking at this CRM phenomenon in light of the drivers of banking innovation since the 1970s, one might wonder if CRM itself is the innovation, or (conversely) the technology, once again. Much is being written about CRM. Bankers at all points of the CRM spectrum are looking for a way to quantify their return on investment—either what it actually is or, if just starting out, what it should be and over what period of time should the value be realized. Ironically, the answer to this question may lie in a simple review of a few known qualities generated from historical innovation.

Look, for example, at ATMs. What drove many bankers to invest in ATMs was the promise of reduced branch cost, since customers would use them instead of a branch to transact business. But what was discovered is that the financial impact of ATMs is a marginal increase in fee income substantially offset by the cost of significant increases in the number of customer transactions. The value proposition, however, was a significant increase in that intangible called customer satisfaction. The increase in customer satisfaction has translated to loyalty that resulted in higher customer retention and growing franchise value.

Internet banking, a product of the 1990s shows similar characteristics. Again, bankers invested believing that the Internet was a lower-cost delivery channel and a way to increase sales. Studies have now shown, however, that the primary value of offering Internet banking services lies in the increased retention of highly valued customer segments. Again, the intangible called customer satisfaction drives the value proposition. Now we explore CRM. CRM is not another ATM or Internet bank. It is not a checking account, a stock or a mortgage.

CRM is primarily driven by the innovation of technology, but unlike other technological innovation, CRM has power to help bankers quickly and directly improve customer satisfaction. CRM is an added dimension to ensure that what the customer expects is consistent with what the bank is prepared to deliver. One expert in bank CRM initiatives recently said that CRM is an approach that is less focused on providing the right services to the customer than attracting customers who are the right fit for what the bank has to offer. Further, the primary value of CRM is its potential as a customer retention tool. People are starting to measure CRM in terms of increased customer satisfaction. Rather than Return on Investment.

## CRM IN THE BANKING SECTOR—AN EXPERIENCE

The last decade has seen many changes taking place in the structure of banking and also in the way the Banking sector has opened up. Deregulation and entry of new players are changing the Banking scene. To say that the future belongs to a particular group, Private Banks or Foreign Banks or Public sector Banks is not correct. The future belongs to the player who keeps in touch with the time, who moves along with the time and is able to respond to the emerging needs of the customers.

Today Banking is changing we are seeing technology being introduced in the sector. A greater amount of dis-intermediation is taking place in the higher segment of the corporate sector and there is a need for providing better quality customer service. The market is becoming more and more buyer dominated. In Banking, the final result as to who will actually be able to woo customers will depend on their ability to react and respond to the customer requirement. The customer is going to be the real decider of fate of Banks.

The Banks want to be a major retail consumer Banks in India. The part of retail Banking goes not only with Credit Card but Debit Cards and Smart Cards as well. The Customer can get a bunch of additional services with co-branded cards, which have tie-ups with petroleum Co's, airlines, hospital chains. Banks have introduced Debit Cards self-explanatory card that caters very well to the tastes of credit averse Indians. The banks are providing all products under one roof and that includes the retail staff as well.

HDFC Bank, ICICI, UTI Bank and HSBC, City are wooing corporate to open salary accounts. The minimum balance required for these accounts is zero and hence customer base of these Banks is exponentially increasing. ATM network, which provides visibility and convenience and hence helps in increase customer acquisition, is set near railway station, petrol pump, shopping complexes, etc.

Internet Banking is available to the customer at his desktop, while the branches may be 2 to 3 kms away. Some banks have already ventured to maintain relationship with online banking through Internet. The latest trend in banking strategy is clicks and bricks in which customer can debit or credit accounts, check balances and even trade on it. A car loan is other area in which banks are developing relationship with the customer. The ideal model of maintainining relationship with the customer focuses on the customer service issues. Banks are providing customers with the highest quality services with special emphasis on recognizing customer needs and cross selling (expanding relationship with existing clients to increase range of services delivered to the clients) appropriate bank services. In a nutshell the customer has become the fulcrum of all Banking activities.

## BANKING INDUSTRY : FOCUS ON CRM

CRM means that fundamental decisions on strategy and resource allocation must be based on a detailed and accurate understanding of customers and the overall market. It feels that customized CRM solutions can provide access to the information you need to come out on top. The customizable CRM solution can:

- Integrate information from multiple sources, eliminate data errors and redundancies, tailor data for efficient access and analysis, and reduce the complexity of data management.
- Anticipate customer expectations and predict customer behavior like, propensity to purchase, lifetime profitability, and credit risk.
- Allow to cross-sell and up-sell. It can help identify the best candidates for purchasing particular combinations of products and services, and focus the marketing efforts on a more receptive audience.
- Combine business rules and analytic models to accurately segment and profile customers, and construct a personalized strategy for each group.
- Deliver customer intelligence into front office systems to enable smarter customer interactions through various channels.
- Combine behavioral insights derived from analytics with attitudinal data obtained from online and offline customer surveys.

The primary business driver of message-based middleware solutions in the banking industry is Customer Relationship Management, the business of customer acquisition, customer development and customer retention:

| **Customer Lifecycle** | Customer Acquisition → | Customer Development → | Customer Retention |
|---|---|---|---|
| **Strategic Question** | Who are the profitable Customer and how to We attract them? | How do we deliver what customers want, how they want it, when they want it? | How do we build and sustain customer Loyalty? |
| **Objective and Value** | *Efficient targeting of Profitable Customer<br>*High hit rate<br>*Marketing and sales Effectiveness | *Effective Product service design and delivery<br>*Customer Satisfaction<br>*Increasing share of Cross Selling | *Lifetime Relationship<br>*Increased Profitability |

## CRM IN BANKS—A FUTURE VIEW

For long, Indian banks had presumed that their operations were customer-centric, simply because they had customers. These banks ruled the roost, protected by regulations that did not allow free entry into the sector. And to their credit, when the banking sector was opened up, they survived by adapting quickly to the new rules of the game. Many managed to post profits. For them an unexpected bonanza came from government bonds in which most were hugely invested.

The Reserve Bank of India's moves to cut aggressively the interest rates after 1999 pushed up the prices of bonds. So banks had a windfall doing almost nothing. The bond profits, like manna from heaven, improved the balance sheets of all banks irrespective of their core performance. However, the era of lazy banking is soon to end. The mesh of rules that propped up the Indian banking industry is now being dismantled rapidly.

According to a RBI road map, India will have a competitive banking market after 2009. As one of the most attractive emerging market destinations, India will see foreign banks come in, what with more freedom to come in, grow and acquire. Therefore, it is imperative that Indian banks wake up to this reality and re-focus on their core asset—the customer. A greater focus on Customer Relationship Management (CRM) is the only way the banking industry can protect its market share and boost growth.

CRM would also make Indian bankers realise that the purpose of their business is to "create and keep a customer" and to "view the entire business process as consisting of a tightly integrated effort to discover, create, and satisfy customer needs."

CRM is, probably, one of the least clearly defined business acronyms, as there is no single definition for it. It is probably easier to say what CRM is not. Unfortunately, CRM has also become a misnomer for a range of solutions from IT vendors, each providing its own spin on the idea. CRM is variously misunderstood as a fancy sales strategy, an expensive software product, or even a new method of data collection. It is none of these. CRM is a simple philosophy that places the customer at the heart of a business organization's processes, activities and culture to improve his satisfaction of service and, in turn, maximize the profits for the organization.

A successful CRM strategy aims at understanding the needs of the customer and integrating them with the organization's strategy, people, technology and business process. Therefore, one of the best ways of launching a CRM initiative is to start with what the organization is doing now and working out what should be done to improve its interface with its customers. Then and only then, should it link to an IT solution?

While this may sound quite straightforward, for large organisations it can be a mammoth task unless a gradual step-by-step process is adopted. It does not happen simply by buying the software and installing it. For CRM to be truly effective, it requires a well-thought-out initiative involving strategy, people, technology, and processes. Above all, it requires the realisation that the CRM philosophy of doing business should be adopted incrementally with an iterative approach to learn at every stage of development. Only time will tell how Indian banks embrace the CRM philosophy and take on the competition from foreign entities.

## CONCULSION

Customer relationship management as an integral part of the overall business strategy. Customer relationship management is a complex process because it raises the host of challenging business issues that lie at the interface of both Finance and Marketing. The forces of deregulation, globalization and advancing technology have increased the competitive pressure in the banking industry.

The Indian banking industry too is going through turbulent times. Since the financial reforms started, banks have been given a great degree of freedom in determining their rate structure for deposit and advances as well as their product range. The freedom of choice, which bank customers, did not have earlier because of standardized products and regimented interest rates have now been given to the customers. Thus, in this era of increased competition, in order to proper, it has now become imperative for the bank to focus on developing long-term relationships with their customers.

## References

Chaturvedi, 'Customer Relationship Management', EXL Publications, New Delhi.

Shainesh, 'Customer Relationship Management', MAC Publications, New Delhi.

Mahammed, 'Customer Relationship Management', Vikas Publications, New Delhi.

Kincaid, 'Customer Relationship Management', Pearson Publications.

Das, 'Customer Relationship Management', UNK Publications.

http: / / www.sap.com / industries / banking / pdf / BWP_CRM_banking.pdf

http: / / www.erpweb.com / crm.htm

# Factors Leading to Non-Performing Assets and Recovery Measures

M. SUMATHY

## INTRODUCTION

Today's Banking scenario has undergone tremendous change. Banks give loans to various individuals trade and industry sector. The entire banking system is systematically meeting the various credit needs of our society. At the same time, the safety of the advance also counts a lot. Bankers have to watch very carefully the recovery process as any failure on their part will lead to accumulation of non-performing asset, popularly known as NPA, in their portfolio. This article attempts to recall the factors that lead to NPA and the recovery measures. Though much has been said and written about this topic, the purpose of this article is to serve as a capsule for the students of Banking and Bankers to refer to the vital points at any point of time in connection with non-performing assets.

## MAIN FACTORS LEADING TO NPAS

There are two factors—External and Enternal that leads to NPAs. The main points under each head are discussed below:

### External Factors

Raw material shortage is one of the major factors. Due to raw material shortage, production process in any industry gets hampered and loan repayment gets delayed. Power shortage is another aspect. Due to frequent power interruption the production targets cannot be achieved. Sudden and unexpected price escalation also causes strain in the repaying ability of the borrower and Banks face recovery problem under such situation. If any activity is dependent on monsoon, failure of monsoon will affect the required output. Excess capacities, natural calamities also lead to disruption in the production and this also will cause enormous problems.

India is a country with multi-various culture and languages. Social disparities and social unrest will affect the free movement of products from one place to another which will ultimately land in instability of production and naturally tremendous pressure on the borrowers to repay the borrowed money. Further the policies of the Government also holds a lot of importance as far as the banking system is concerned and any undue changes in the policy shall also affect the repaying ability of the borrower.

*Internal factors*: The internal factors can be of two types—borrower specific and bank-specific. Under borrower-specific caption, the following are the important factors:

(a) *Management inefficiency*: Everything centers around the Management. If the Management is inefficient and ineffective, naturally the industry will fail.

(b) *Diversion of funds and misutilisation of funds*: The money borrowed is to be used for the purpose for which it has been lent. Any diversion and improper utilization shall lead to NPA.

(c) *Faulty project planning resulting in time/cost over run or wrong technology*: Technology is one of the main aspects in Modern society. If the project is not planned effectively and wrong technology measures are adopted that will lead to unnecessary problems.

(d) *Failure to capture market*: If the product fails to capture market, then sales will be down and as such profit will dip and the Bank loan will not be repaid.

(e) *Strained labour relations*: If there is labour problem in any industry it will lead to strained relationship with the management and production will stop and that is enough for the failure of the advance.

(f) *Wilful default*: Another factor is wilful default by the borrower. He may have sufficient capacity to repay but he is not paying.

(g) *Product obsolescence*: If the product becomes old and outdated, the sales will go down and the account becomes NPA.

**Internal—Bank-Specific**

*Too many eggs in one basket*: If there is concentration of only in one type of advance, failure in that will land in trouble for the entire portfolio.

Inadequate credit analysis, adverse selection of the customer also cause problems. Competition is another factor. Besides incomplete documentation, non-renewal of document in time also create failure in accounts. Failure to recogonise warning signals will turn the account into NPA. Hence it is necessary on the part of the banker to watch carefully for the warning signals like non-submission of financial statements in time, non-renewal of proposals, late submission or non-submission of stock statements, frequent request for exceeding the sanctioned limit and the like. Here the Banker has to remember the famous saying of Martin Luther King which says—

For want of a nail a shoe was lost;
For want of a shoe a horse was lost;
For want of a horse a soldier was lost;
For want of a soldier a battle was lost.

Hence it is needed that small things are also given proper attention to protect the account from turning into NPA.

Other factors include an excessive reliance on collaterals. Customers are to be contacted frequently. Infrequent customer contact will lead to loss of touch and that will cause more problems.

*Loan review mechanism*: This can also be called as LRM. More care has to be exercised by the banker in monitoring the advances given. Poor control over loan documentation, failure to improve collaterals as credit quality deteriorate—all lead to failed review loan mechanism—leading to NPA.

*Measures for recovery*: This is of two types. Non legal and legal measures.

*Non-legal measures*: For effective recovery non-legal measures like the following to be adhered to by the Bankers.

1. *Reminder system*: Reminding the customers in time for repaying the dues to the bank will help the banker as well as the customer to keep a track of the respective loan portfolio and will arrest the possibility of the loan turning into NPA.
2. *Visit to the borrower's office or residence*: Prompt visit to the borrower place will help in having a personal talk with the client and have a close follow up.
3. *Appointment of professional agency*: People or agencies that possess training and expertise in recovery process can be appointed for quick recovery.
4. Recovery cam can be conducted frequently.
5. Rehabilitation of sick units may be initiated by rescheduling the terms of repayment, sanction terms, etc.
6. Corporate Debt Restructure body can be approached in cases of eligible corporate advances causing financial strain regarding recovery.
7. Lokadalat can be approached.
8. Defaulters list can be circulated among the bankers.
9. Appropriation of the subsidy can be done.
10. Right to sell of can be exercised properly.
11. The advances can be recalled in time.
12. The expertise of the specialized branches can be used for recovery mechanism.

**Legal Measures**

In this comes the following:

Recovery through judicial process.

Debt Recovery tribunal can be approached for settling the dues to the banks.

National Company law tribunal can also be approached for this purpose.

The Government frequently talks on merger and amalgamation. By dong so, recovery measures can be speeded up as the geographical and regional coverage will be more.

Financial reconstruction measures may be adopted wherever possible.

Recovery through securitsation and reconstruction of financial assets and Enforcement of securities interest act can also be done.

## CONCLUSION

In a nut shell NPA is a double edged sword. It affects the profitability of the bank and no further interest can be debited once the account is classified and recovery becomes very difficult as days pass on. Hence clear cut recovery mechanism is to be adopted by the banks and it is very essential that only quality advance are always considered and no undue political or any other pressure to be yielded as banks deal in Public money.

# 8

# Customer Relationship Management [CRM] and E-CRM in Banks

## Need of the Hour

M. BALASUNDARAM AND M. SUMATHY

## PROLOGUE

CRM—Customer Relationship Management can be defined as the strategies, processes, people and technologies used by companies to successfully attract and retain customers for maximum corporate growth and profit. CRM initiatives are designed with the goal of meeting customer expectations and needs in order to achieve maximum customer lifetime value and return to the enterprise. The use of customer relationship management products, CRM software and CRM solutions will enhance the effective implementation of CRM in an organization. In simpler terms, CRM is the technique of establishing and maintaining long-term business relationships with your customers. CRM involves utilizing the data collected during your customer interactions to determine the demographics and future needs of each customer.

## WHAT IS THE GOAL OF CRM?

The idea of CRM is that it helps businesses use technology and human resources to gain insight into the behaviour of customers and the value of those customers. With an effective CRM strategy, a business can increase revenues by:

- providing services and products that are exactly what your customers want
- offering better customer service
- cross selling products more effectively
- helping sales staff close deals faster
- retaining existing customers and discovering new ones

Banks in India are catering to all financial requirements of customers. CRM involves various measures combining innovation, quality, personal touch and flexibility in delivery. While getting customers is fundamental to business success, retaining customer is more important. Banks work to build long-term relationships with their customers. The term relationship management communicates the idea that a major goal of a business enterprise is to engage in interactions with customers over the long-term. A principle theme of customer relationship management is to attract, retain and keep the customers satisfied. Satisfied customers develop positive interactions and visit the banks more frequently and introduce more new quality customers. As Banks strive to treat to customers in a manner that encourages repeat business, they maximize lifetime value of the customer relationships. Banks know that their customers who are most satisfied prefer to do business repeatedly with them and the organization they trust. They know that establishing relationships with customers can increase long-run business reduce marketing costs. Any business enterprise must focus on getting and retaining customers.

## CRM IMPLEMENTATION

CRM—Customer relationship management is a corporate level strategy, focusing on creating and maintaining relationships with customers. Several commercial CRM software packages are available which vary in their approach to CRM. However, CRM is not a technology itself, but rather a holistic approach to an organization's philosophy, placing the emphasis firmly on the customer. CRM governs an organization's philosophy at all levels, including policies and processes, front of house customer service, employee training, marketing, systems and information management. CRM systems are integrated end-to-end across marketing, sales, and customer service. There are three fundamental components in CRM Operational CRM automation of basic business processes (marketing, sales, and service).

- Analytical CRM—analysis of customer data and behaviour using business intelligence.
- Collaborative CRM—communicating with clients.

### Uses of CRM

CRM covers all interaction and business with customers. A good CRM program allows a business to acquire customers, provide customer services and retain valued customers. CRM can improve Customer services by:

- CRM providing a mechanism for handling problems and complaints.
- CRM providing a mechanism for correcting service deficiencies.
- CRM Storing customer interests in order to target customers selectively.
- CRM providing mechanisms for managing and scheduling maintenance, repair, and on-going support.

- CRM providing online access to product information and technical assistance around the clock.
- CRM identifying what customer's value and devising appropriate service strategies for each customer.
- CRM providing mechanisms for managing and scheduling follow-up sales calls.
- CRM Tracking all contacts with a customer.
- CRM Identifying potential problems before they occur.
- CRM providing a user-friendly mechanism for registering customer complaints.

Relationship management addresses the need of marketing and its desire to improve profitability and satisfies lifetime needs of the customers better than the competitor. At a tactical level, when inappropriately applied, relationship management uses information technology to spawn short-term loyalty schemes that are often opportunistic and may create loyalty to the incentive. Thus it is important to understand both the philosophy and tactics of custbmer relationship management. A customer relationship management system is a process to compile information that increases understanding of how to manage an organization's relationship with its customers. This system consists of two dimensions, analysis and action.

More formally, customer relationship management is a business strategy that uses information technology to provide an enterprise with a comprehensive, reliable and integrated view of its customer base so that all process and customer interactions help maintain and expand mutually beneficial relationships. Customer relationship management is thus a technique designed to collect data and provide information that helps the organizations to evaluate strategic options. A customer relationship management strategy should help organizations to improve the profitability of their interactions with current and potential customers. While at the same time making those interactions appear friendlier through individualization and personalization.

The purpose of a customer relationship management is to enhance customer service, improve customer satisfaction and ensure customer retention by aligning business processes with technology integration. A customer relationship management brings us together lots of prices of information about customer, customer characteristics, sales transactions, marketing effectiveness, responsiveness and marketing trends. An effective customer relationship management system describes customer relationships in sufficient detail so that all aspects of the organization can access information, match customer needs with satisfying product offering, remind customers of service requirements, know what others products customers have been purchased in the past, and so forth.

## IMPORTANCE OF THE STUDY

One of the ongoing challenges successful businesses face is in optimizing customer satisfaction and developing customer relationship management. So many companies "jump on the bandwagon" of improving customer service in order to impact customer retention levels. Companies that need customers in order to build a profit need to have a system in place that effectively and successfully manages the customer relationship. Banking institutions today face many challenges including global competition for deposits, loans and underwriting fees: increasing customer demands; shrinking profit margins; and the need to keep up with new technologies. To encounter these obstacles strong customer relationships is required. This relationship depends on ability to provide personalized service to every customer, every time, everywhere.

With help of effective customer relationship management a bank can improve the quality of sales and service at every touch point, including branch offices, kiosks, ATMs, call centers, fax, Internet, e-mail and direct marketing. Today, a handful of retail banks can boast of globally integrated delivery channels that are built on standard technology principles. These channels can, for example, deliver consistent balances regardless of the customer's location because of the consistent architecture. No institution, however, can claim to have all channels working on a common platform or claim even to share information or process across all channels. IT managers within the bank, as well as business managers that rely on the delivery channels to service their products, know deep down that integrating the channels is the right thing to do because some benefits of channel integration are intuitive if not scientifically provable.

Banks are governed by Banking Regulations Act, 1949, RBI Act, 1932, and Negotiable Instruments Act, 1881. Goi Poria Committee was formed to improve customer service. Quick and prompt service is the motto of all banks today. It is the customers who command the banking industry. Small customers/villages understood the need of savings. Hence many banks have come into picture in today's market. As days roll on, the demands of the customers keep changing. Banks have to play the role of a super market measure providing various financial services under the roof. Under such circumstances, customer relationship is very important. Bringing in a customer, giving him good service, satisfying his banking needs and retaining him is a tough task. This is a very important point on part of the banks. That is why the concept of Know Your Customer (KYC) has been introduced. If the bankers know their customers, naturally service improves. If service improves, relationship improves. If relationship improves, business improves. If business improves, profitability improves. If profit improves, economy improves. If economy improves, our status in global scenario improves. This is what the Government and the people are striving for.

## E-CRM MEGA TRENDS

*Imagine this e-CRM scenario*: A customer visits a bricks and mortar store and registers at a kiosk. Later, at home, the customer receives a "thank you for visiting" e-mail along with a special offer. Intrigued, the customer clicks on the hyperlink to the online store, gets friendly advice from a virtual shopping assistant and designs his or her own wardrobe. A few days later, the customer is alerted by a dynamically generated phone call that a preferred sweater style has become available. The customer makes a purchase by pressing keys on the phone keypad and picks up the package from the store that evening. This scenario highlights three key trends of the e-CRM movement:

(1) Every business is becoming an information business
(2) Direct marketing is increasingly important
(3) The growth of "the Value Exchange"—non-commercial interactions between customers and companies.
(4) These are eCRM Mega trends.

**Trend 1: Every Business is an Information Business**

In addition to deriving value from physical goods and services, consumers increasingly value information. Amazon.com value proposition to customers includes community forums for various literary and musical subsets. Each forum includes recommendations from like-minded individuals, reader reviews, and interviews with authors and artists and other useful information. EBay, Priceline.com and E-LOAN have also emerged as new information-value-based businesses. Traditional bricks and mortar businesses have begun to follow suit. Toys R Us, the large toy retailer, has significantly increased the information intensity of its value proposition to customers. In addition to buying toys, customers can check out product reviews from a web site, sign up for email reminders for birthdays or track their order status. In the healthcare industry, one health maintenance organization introduces individuals with chronic health conditions to virtual communities of other patients and experts. In the entertainment industry, a major video retailer emails personalized news and information about upcoming movies, events and fan club material to customers based on their rental preferences. Not just in retail and healthcare, but across the board, in industries ranging from manufacturing to financial services, information intensity is increasing as part of businesses' value propositions to customers

**Trend 2: Ascendancy of Direct Marketing**

Strong brands will always be important, but brands will be built increasingly through direct one-to-one marketing.

Mass marketing compresses an economic signal indicating a value propo ,ition. Why compress a value proposition when unlimited bandwidth is available to personalize and amplify that message for each potential customer? Inexpensive multi-media, multi-channel offer presentment and integrated campaign analysis capability make the economics of direct marketing superior to "one size fits all" marketing efforts. Significant redirection of marketing spending is at hand. A recent study of the automobile industry by Mckinsey and company suggests that, in the near future, direct marketing efforts will consume 80% of all marketing spending

**Trend 3: The Value Exchange**

The Value Exchange is a mutually beneficial exchange of valued information between a company and its customers. Both parties give and receive information that is valuable to the other and in the process, build a lasting relationship. For example, P&G sponsors a web site devoted to parental concerns on child rearing. From the ongoing dialog on parenting, P&G gains valuable information on customer's product concerns, demographics and buying habits. This information enhances P&G's decisions on product features, promotions and pricing for Pampers and other child care products. In the Value Exchange model, 90% of customers/ company interactions are information transfers, only 10% are transactions. The Value Exchange is an emerging dominant business practice in the Internet Age. Email, cell phones, Net TV, WAP phones and data-driven automated broadcasting make it possible to generate hundreds of millions of personalized touches per day at low cost .

CRM involves all these steps by collecting the personal information of a customer; banks can create a data base. By getting the photo, identity is established. By getting the address proof, address is established. By collecting the other details, the main aspects of the customers are revealed. Once that is done, a smooth relationship starts between the banker and the customer. CRM acts as a bridge to link the banker and the customer to the society at large.

## THE FIVE ENGINES OF ECRM

Companies understand that eCRM has significant potential, but they face the challenge of building the required technology infrastructure quickly and cost effectively. A knee-jerk reaction is to buy off-the-shelf applications, cobble together a data base of web traffic and online purchase information and launch an eCRM initiative. Unfortunately many such efforts have met with poor results. Recent research indicates that 39% of online shoppers failed in shopping attempts, and a staggering 66% of loaded online shopping carts were abandoned before the checkout process. Less than 5% of unique visitors become customers. A more sound approach is to install a comprehensive software platform of five engines that together enable the eCRM business process. These five engines are:

1. *The Customer-centric Information Store*—
   To consolidate information about millions of customers together with preferences, permissions and information that may be useful to them.
2. *The Analysis and Segmentation Engine*—
   To leverage this customer information to build a business campaign strategy and evaluate its success.
3. *The Personalization Engine*—
   To personalize the entire customer experience, configuring unique sets of messages and offers to each customer.
4. *The Broadcast Engine*—
   To proactively deliver information and offers to every customer via the media of his or her choice.
5. *The Transaction Engine*—
   To facilitate the interactions between customer and the company, either exchanging information or driving transactions properly configured, these five engines collectively form a robust, scalable and flexible platform for eCRM. Both prefabricated and custom-made software can be seamlessly integrated into the platform to provide a virtual shopkeeper to millions of customers. Equipped with such

infrastructure, companies can continually create significant customer value at Internet speed, who, what, when, where and how of sales and marketing.

## CONCLUSION

CRM stands for Customer Relationship Management. It is a process or methodology used to learn more about customers' needs and behaviours in order to develop stronger relationships with them. There are many technological components to CRM, but thinking about CRM in primarily technological terms is a mistake. The more useful way to think about CRM is as a process that will help bring together lots of pieces of information about customers, sales, marketing effectiveness, responsiveness and market trends. CRM helps businesses use technology and human resources to gain insight into the behaviour of customers and the value of those customers.

An effective customer relationship management system describes customer relationships in sufficient detail so that all aspects of the organization can access information, match customer needs with satisfying product offering, remind customers of service requirements, know what others products customers have been purchased in the past, and so forth. The eCRM tsunami has begun and executives in every major company will have to formulate and execute an eCRM strategy rapidly in order to keep up with competition. Since eCRM is an enterprise-wide phenomenon, senior executives and general mangers drive these activities in most companies. This white paper was created to clarify critical technology issues on eCRM in understandable terms without compromising accuracy.

### REFERENCES

Hall, W.K., "Survival Strategies in a Hostile Environment", *Harvard Business Review*, 1988.

Indian Banking Challenges Ahead, *Yojana*, Feb. 2001.

http://www.indiawebdevelopers.com/articles/ecrm_solutions.asp

http://www.microstrategy.com/Download/files/whitepapers/ecrm23.pdf

# APPENDIX

## CRM Wheel

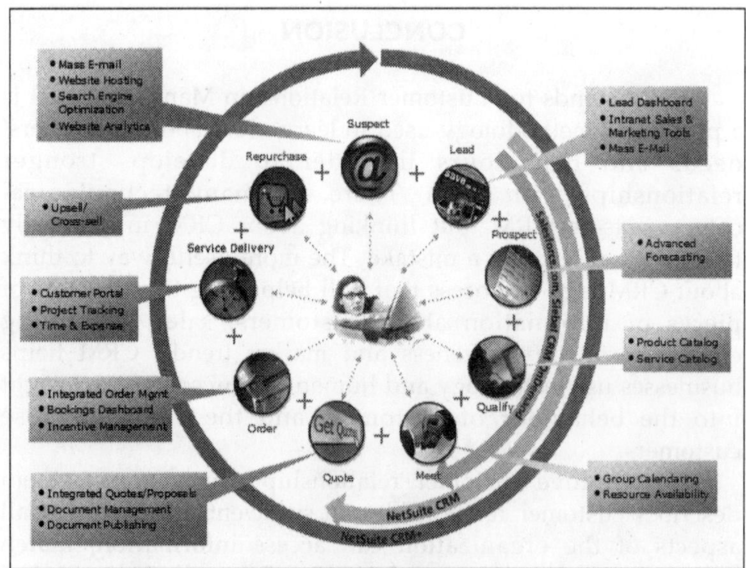


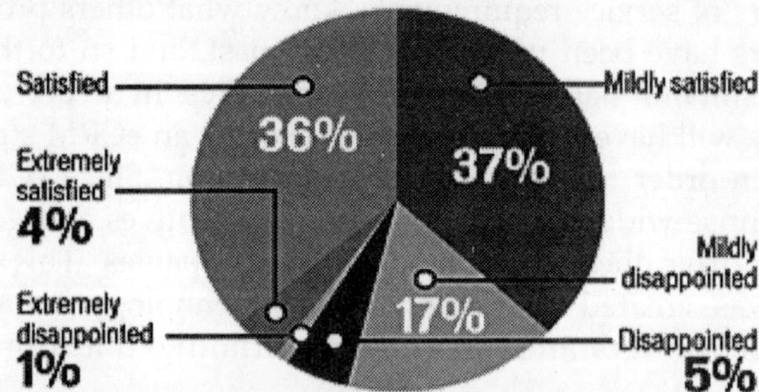


**From a quick and easy software solution for a small business**

**To a Comprehensive Enterprise Solution**

# 9

# *Strategic Management of Human Resources and the Challenge of Employee Attrition in Organizations*

M. Basheer Ahmed Khan and
Swaroop Chandra Sahoo

## ABSTRACT

In a facilitating environment the world over, private players have emerged in an unprecedented way to establish entrepreneurial ventures. In the struggle to start up, stabilize, sustain, succeed and surge ahead, the establishments should have organizational capability which can provide it the needed competitive edge. Needless to state that organization is people and the quality of organization will depend on the quality of its human resources. The organizations get just destabilized when they face problems of employee turn over and attrition. Short-term measures to lure the employees are taken by many organizations. But, what is the best way to manage the human resources of the organizations? What is strategic human resources management and how is it used to address the concerns of employees attrition in organizations? This paper makes an attempt to understand conceptually and practically the issues involved and provides the example through a case as to how strategic management of human resources is used to manage employee attrition and enhancing the employee productivity. A customized replication of such efforts will go a long way in addressing the HR concerns of organizations in the newly emerged competitive environment.

## I. INTRODUCTION

The business environment the world over is in a flux and the only consensus is that what is constant in this given environment is the frequent change. In such an environment, all firms globally face a profound challenge of how to leverage the human capital to gain competitive advantage for the individual firms. To face this challenge, the strategic impact of human resources and the dynamic framework it delivers to enable the organization to quickly adapt to changing conditions and seize new opportunities as they emerge is a matter of common interest. Human Resources Management, hence is viewed from the angle of a strategic approach to employment,[1] especially when the employees are on move causing yet another concern of managing the rate of employee attrition in the organizations. Competitive and free market environment throws up opportunities for entrepreneurs to start, multiply and enlarge organizations. But the organizations can get started, survive, stabilize, succeed and surge ahead only if they have the right kind of human resources. The management challenge, hence, is acquiring the right human resources and retaining them from a long-term point of view, not withstanding the fact that some human resources will always turn over as a natural process. A strategic human resources management with appropriate built in mechanism to address issues of attrition can bring several advantages to the organization. It is indeed a challenge and the success of management depends on the success of retaining its competent human resources over a long period of time.

## II. STRATEGIC HUMAN RESOURCES MANAGEMENT

As Prof. O'Reilli opines, the Managers who have a strategic management perspective today must be effective at simultaneously monitoring current performance, managing incremental innovation, and leading more revolutionary or discontinuous change efforts. The Human Resources for the Strategic Advantage program of any organization should explore how to manage this delicate balancing act by emphasizing methods to align HR strategy with the overall business strategy. The concern that needs to be addressed in such situations would be, how to strategically utilize human resource levers—such as culture, compensation, and performance management—to build competitive advantage and drive the organization to success. In their effort to address such concerns, the top management should succeed in three major areas such as:

- Evolving concepts and frameworks that would help directly link human resources with the organization's vision and competitive strategy,
- Evolving and managing human resource policies and practices in ways that add the most value to the organization, and
- Implementing change and managing organizational transition as the organization adapts to new market conditions.

These in turn will help the organization to have a strategic human resources management approach to employment ensuring retention of its talents and managing the possible attrition to a level which will be within the tolerance threshold of the organization. However, in spite of the fact that human resource management has gained popular and wide usage, as a concept for managing employment (from its traditional view of personnel management), to a great extent the practices do not convey a clear concept. As Chris Hendry (1995)[2] writes, "HRM has different connotations for different people and does not yet constitute a unified theory. We are all familiar with such statements as 'our human resources are our most important asset'. In some cases, acceptance of the principles of HRM goes no further than this. Others emphasize that it is about matching employment practices to an organization's strategy. A corollary of this is that, taken as a whole employment practices should combine together to reinforce one another. Part of this is that employment decisions should not be conceived in isolation, but ideally should be integrated through mechanisms such as personnel planning. At the same time, reward systems, the way promotions are made, who gets trained and why, all have effects on motivation and say something about what kind of organization it is and what behaviours it wants to promote."[3] Hence, an effective human resources management should be able to speak aloud the distinctive philosophy of the organization in acquiring, engaging, inspiring, rewarding, retaining, rehabilitating the human resources from a strategic point of view that it is able to secure the commitment and motivation of its people who will intertwine their personnel growth with the growth of the organization and will be continuing to participate and identify with the organization for a possible long period of time.

Human Resources Management in organizations has been discussed for its conceptual issues. Alfred Chandler (1962),[4] for instance, discussed that structure should follow strategy so that the organization remains more efficient.

Predominance of human resources management was emphasized by Galbraith and Nathanson (1978)[5] suggesting that human resources management system should be adapted to meet the requirements of strategy. Fombrun, Tichy and Devanna (1984)[6] added the elements that would empower the personnel policy.

According to Guest (1987)[7] there are four goals which can be specifically measured to evaluate human resources management. These goals are the development of employee commitment, the flexibility that the employees can pursue, the quality performance of the employees through high quality employees and the strategic integration of people with policies. These goals can be the elements of HRM which are measurable. Within the contours of these goals, the strategic management of people and personnel systems and the innovations carried out to promote employee commitment have become more prominent. Employee involvement and commitment are two essential elements of employee's emotional attachment to the organization and the resultant retention. However, such policies have not been taken lightly by the experts of industrial relations as it was considered that policies involving individual employees will be perceived as efforts to side track the trade unions (Kochan and Capelli, 1984;[8] Guest, 1992).[9] Involving individual employees both emotionally and from the point of view of mutual benefit of the organization and the individual employee will necessarily create more employee commitment. The resultant lowered interest in trade unions may be a consequence. After all, if the trade unions are for the benefit of the employees and if the organizations attend to the benefits directly, the employees need not feel peeved and trade unionists need not feel hurt. If the trade unionists are interested in only politicizing employee benefits, it is better that the trade unions are handled accordingly. Commitment to the organization so developed needs to be sustained through a regular and continuous strategy and policy of the organization to function with the psychologically involved support of the employees rather than something imposed on the employees. Such a policy has to be put in place through the human resources management in areas more specifically as recruitment, selection, socialization, organization-specific training, team-building, network of communications, etc. The managers need to build in appropriate methodologies to use these HR elements in a strategic perspective.

The strategic perspective has to be fully analyzed to implement utilizing appropriate skills. The strategy has to be at perceptual level and then at practical level. There are differences in strategy perceptions and practices. Most organizations perceive about a corporate strategy and the HR practice will be presumed to be in harmony with the corporate strategy. However, this need not be so with all organizations. The corporate strategy is basically conceived at the Board level and is a matter of interest of the top managers, while strategic management of the HR is always left to the lower level managers. This leads to a mismatch and impracticality in many areas.

The strategic management of the organization need not and does not many times remain realistic to consider the operational level issues. It is said that employees who quit organizations do not quit the organizations *per se*, but they leave their managers. Why should this happen if strategic management of the organizations intertwine the strategic human resources management aspects also and both addressed at the top level as an organizational commitment?

Ansoff (1965)[10] believed that the external environment is controllable by mechanisms of planning the managerial activities. This post-war perception was akin to the thoughts (Knights and Morgan, 1991)[11] that the internal dynamics of the people can be tampered with the systems developed. As a result, the rational and analytical models were developed for formulating strategy. Some such examples are the models like TOWS, PIMS portfolio and M. Porter's. Following the building of these models, it was believed that strategy making will be explicit, deliberate and based on a top-down approach. However, in practicing strategic management, it was observed that strategy is not deliberate and it "emerges" after the event (Mintzberg, 1987)[12] and it is better that strategic management is allowed to be so without a rigid segregation of strategy of the top and the operation at the bottom. Many other writers have also delved on these issues. It is generally viewed that the process and content of strategy are equally important human resources management and hence, have to be knitted with the strategic management with a long-term perspective for developing the people of the organization at all levels and create an organizational climate and culture for the continuous development of the people. This continuous development will require people to be with the organization for long and be the result of a long-term policy of retaining its people. The strategic human resources management will orient its actions from this perspective of retaining the people and managing the possible attrition to have the people sharing the organizational benefit and making them contribute to the organizational benefits. This possibility can be ensured only with a built up of organizational capability by acquiring and retaining competent and high performance human resources. Building organizational capability is a pre-requisite for the competitive advantage of the organization. Strategic management theorists also view this as such. (Ulrich and Lake, 1990;[13] Nelson, 1991;[14] Porter, 1991).[15] The static approach to competitive advantage over looks the importance of strategy implementation. Strategic Human Resources Management is realistic about the need for building organizational capability and the competitive advantage for the organization and for this, it takes an approach of long-term planning of employees, their retention and management of attrition.

## III. THE CHALLENGE OF EMPLOYEE ATTRITION

In the absence of such strategic management of human resources, employee attrition has become a critical issue for many organizations. The short-term arrangement of acquiring employees and engaging them with short-sighted rewards have been causing havocs in the organizational management with many of the industries facing attrition. "Employee retention often focuses more on compensation issues than education and flexible work arrangements. Departing employees take with them valuable knowledge. And lessons learned are not regularly captured or integrated into decision-making. This workforce-planning environment produces fragmented practices that hinder the ability . . . to achieve optimal outcomes. A new workforce-planning approach is needed—an approach that strives to ensure that employees have the right information at the right time to make the right decisions".[16] A facilitating environment for private players with liberalized framework the globe over has seen a sudden spurt of entrepreneurial activities. Employees are the back bone of these organizations and given a free play, the employees also seek better pastures in the absence of any employment safety or rewards for their contribution. With attrition taking a toll, the organizations are loosing their competitive advantage because of weak organizational capability. The challenge is addressed by the organizations through many different managerial tactics of a short-term nature, while the organizations which are entrenched in strategic management are able to hold the employees which are their forte. Strategic actions can be undertaken even if they are not visualized as

HR driven. In a case where such initiative was taken, perceptible results were achieved. In the case[17] reported, an experimental program was launched to manage the challenge of attrition. After careful planning (which is a part of strategic management) and subsequent execution, the organizational dynamics was revolutionized by empowering the key employees (competent employees) to change the organizational culture. IT services organizations struggle to retain and motivate their employees and deliver on tough deadlines, while ensuring that employee turnover and attrition remain low. Often, management falls into the trap of throwing money at valued employees instead of getting to the real root of what motivates them.[18] In the company, whose case is quoted here, an experiment was conducted in which the attrition was lowered considerably and personnel productivity among the critical core employee group was increased significantly. 'A 10-year-old, 500-employee strong IT consulting and services company, with offshore development centers in India and overseas offices in all major IT markets made an attempt to address the issue of attrition. There was a good amount of employee movement between offices and at client sites. The organization had a mediocre record of retaining employees. The problem manifested itself in lower productivity and higher friction between management and staff levels. News of this problem was getting out into the market and the organization was finding it difficult to attract talented employees both from the market and from educational campuses. The organization sincerely wanted to change this culture and hence, had to do something substantial—build a program that would very quickly become self-sustaining and not be seen as HR-driven. It had to have buy-in from all of the managers at all offices, then percolate down, generating a serious buzz among staff. The organization wanted something that wouldn't be learned about through the office grapevine or interpreted as hype. The organization had a short time to achieve something measurable. It had to get the objectives and metrics right so that it would know whether it was successful in what it was trying to achieve. It defined objectives from two angles: organizational goals and employee aspirations. It wanted to achieve both and not compromise on either. For organizational aspirations, the following objectives were set:

- To minimize the attrition of those employees whose performance was valued.
- To improve the productivity levels of employees across the board.
- To build a culture where "right attitude" is strongly desirable: Of the three recruitment/promotion requirements of knowledge, skills, and attitude, the organization would award the most weight to attitude, than to knowledge, and finally to skills. This would be a major shift from stressing skills and knowledge and thinking of attitude as "nice to have".

For employee aspirations, it wanted to make sure that it achieved the following:

- A sense of fair play in terms of ensuring that the right employee is given the right reward.
- A way to track and encourage the employees who had the right potential.
- Creation of leadership cadres at all levels: frontline, managerial, and executive.

Before it launched the initiative, it made sure that it had executive sponsorship and support from the board (the top level and middle level commitment, which is a necessary part of strategic management). It also secured expense and time budgeting commitments from division heads. It built feedback and review loops into the normal quarterly business review cycles so that reviews for the program would be inseparable from the more routine business reviews. The Core Program (CP), as it became known, revolved around creating a core of high-performance, high-potential employees who would drive organizational growth, reduce inhibitive factors like attrition, and increase morale. The program was conceived and sustained along the following steps. The organization did an exhaustive, written, form-based survey, which identified five motivators and five inhibitors at the organization, business division, and geographical office levels. With this, it created objectives at a much more granular, relevant-to-business level, as perceived by the employees. In other words, the survey results became the agenda for the Core Program (CP). Then the organization identified the employees from the total employee base who would qualify to be in the CP (Core Program). Those employees who had put in 18 months of service were made eligible for inclusion. The organization felt that it was important for employees to have spent some time understanding the industry and organization-specific business issues so they would be able to play a meaningful role in the Core Program. Core Program criteria identified who among the first level would get into the Core Program. They used the well-known potential-performance grid as a template.

**Employee Potential—Performance Grid**

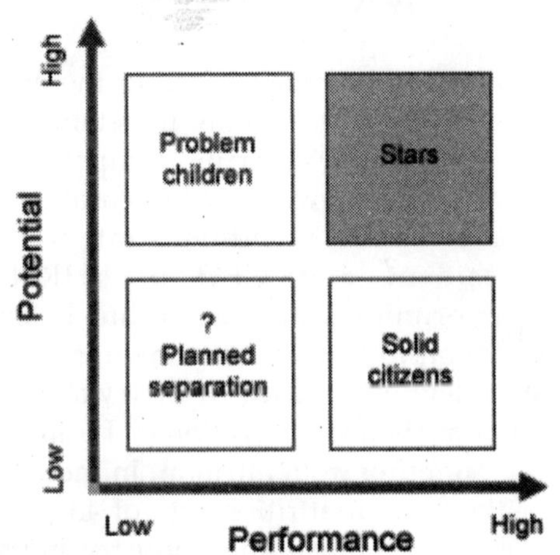


*Source*: Taken from Srinivas Annamaraju, *Ibid*.

It wanted to ensure that the employees inducted into the Core Program would be those who fell in the top-right quadrant. They felt that, while performance speaks to the quality and timeliness of past deliveries, it alone can't be a good enough benchmark, and must be considered with the potential of the individual. For example, a successful regional sales manager (high performer) need not always be a national sales head (with medium potential). In essence, it wanted to ensure that it understood the employee in terms of how well one had done in the past and how successful or versatile one could be in the future. With this, it was arrived at a group of 100 to participate in the Core Program. This exercise helped achieve the organizational goal, individual aspiration and ensured competitive advantage.[19] This in fact was an exercise in strategic human resources management, though it was not christened like SHRM. However, similar planning done from a long range perspective will be strategic human resources management that will not only address reducing attrition, but also ensuring the competitive edge of an organization in an environment of multiple players trying to occupy larger space of the market. This would benefit the employees, organization, competitors and the society if analyzed deeply.

## IV. CONCLUSION

Employee attrition is a major woe to the employers, and organizations are designing systems to retain the employees through many measures. "Offering competitive salaries is important to employees, however, compensation alone is not sufficient for a complete retention strategy", says Susan Meisinger, president and CEO of SHRM.[20] "Career-development opportunities and work/life balance are also important, and employers must consider these types of benefits in their retention practices if they want to maintain or increase retention at their organization".[21] IT and ITES are the major industries suffering from attrition. In India, it is reported that private banks face an attrition rate of 45 per cent among frontline staff. The private insurance industry, in its fourth year of operations in India, has seen an attrition rate in excess of 25 per cent. Some 73 percent of HR executives interviewed in the US said that they were worried about retaining employees. Half of the HR respondents said their employers have implemented special retention programs, up from 35 percent in 2004. Some of the other additional measures adopted by employers are building employee loyalty with HR alternative benefits like flex schedules, free health club memberships and treatment to keep the employees satisfied. Providing that which the employees want is a strategy used by organizations to keep the employees glued to their organization. The various HR practices like pay, power, promotion, perks, position (the 5 Ps of HR) try to woo the employees. Recently, an IT company of repute, the INFOSYS decided to give promotions twice in a year to retain competent employees. But there is a limit to all that can be offered to employees. Even if bench marked facilities are provided and one-up-manship is practiced, attrition is becoming an intractable challenge. But what the organizations should bother is about loosing competent and high performing employees. If the organizations have a strategic human resourcés management program, the practices that would tie up the employees with an organization will be built in as attempted by the organization whose case was referred above. The challenge of attrition of employees can be best addressed by conceptualizing and operationalising the strategic management approach where the corporate strategies and human resources strategies are harmoniously knitted to keep all employees loyal and wedded in general, and high performing employees with the power to establish a congenial culture for the organization. Precepts and practices do support such an approach. The challenge of employee attrition in organization can be best handled if the organizations adopt a human resources management policy with a strategic employment approach.

## Notes and References


1. Chris Hendry, Human Resources Management : A Strategic Approach to Employment, Butterworth Heineman, London, 1995.
2. *Ibid.*
3. *Ibid.*
4. Alfred Chandler, 1962.
5. Galbraith and Nathanson, 1978.
6. Fombrun, Tichy and Devanna, 1984.
7. Guest, 1987.
8. Kochan and Capelli, 1984.
9. Guest, 1982.
10. Guest, 1992.

11. Ansoff, 1965.
12. Knights and Morgan, 1991.
13. Mintzberg, 1987.
14. Ulrich and Lake, 1990.
15. Nelson, 1991.
16. Maria, T. Gresham, Ph.D. and Jeremy Andrulis, IBM Institue for Values, www.ibm.com, 2002.
17. Porter, 1991.
18. Srinivas Annamaraju, "Retention measures trigger new organizational vigor", 2003. This case, as presented by Srinivas is placed in single inverted comas with description converted in indirect sentences with an edited version here for elucidation of the issue in discussion. This case explains how elements of strategic human resources management were introduced without giving the impression that the experiment was HR driven.
19. *Ibid*.
20. www.google.com
21. www.google.com

## References

Aligning Staffing with Business Strategy. TP Bechet, JW Walker—Human Resource Planning, 1993—questia.com.

An Examination of Factors associated with the integration of Human Resources Management and Strategy. N Bennett, D.J. Ketchen Jr., EB Schultz—Human Resource Management, 1998.

Building Knowledge Management into Strategy: Making Sense of a New Perspective S Drew—Long Range Planning, 1999, Elsevier.

Creating Value and Enhancing Retention through Employee Development: The Sun Microsystems Experience. R. Elsdon, S Iyer, Human Resource Planning, 1999—questia.com.

Devolving Human Resource Responsibilities to the Line I. Cunningham, J/ Hyman—Personnel Review, 1999, www. emeraldinsight.com.

Employee Retention: Talent Management; M. Isukapally, AB Academy, Papers.ssm.com.

Human Resource Management: Critical Perspectives on Business and Management, Michael Poole, 2002.

Human Resource Management, J.M. Ivancevich—2001—siricon.com.

Human Resources in Organisations: An Integrated Approach by Rachael Hall, Jim Stewart, Yvonne Leverment, John Leopold, Susan Simpson, Hazel Williams, Diannah Lowry, 2001.

Kushal Vohra, Sr., Systems Approach to Retention of Critical Employees, RAI University, Delhi.

Learn While You Earn: Strategic Management Of The Attrition Problem Within The Indian Bpo Sector Jb Williams.

Management of Call Center-Boredom, Employee Attrition and Retention, A.D. Raina, papers.ssrn.com.

Manpower Planning And Employee Attrition Analytics Raychaudhuri Web Search.

Manpower Retention in IT: An Oxymoron? , S. Tadwalkar and M. Sen, Ubiquity, 2005; portal.ac.org.

Predicting and Managing Turnover in Human Service Agencies: A Case Study of an Organization. D.L. Balfour, D.M. Neff—Public Personnel Management, 1993.

Recruiting and Retaining Employees in a Dynamic Job Market; D.L. Schaeffer, Natural Gas, 1998, doi.wiley.com.

Salary Management/Compensation Strategies, Compensation & Benefits Review.

Strategic Human Resource Management, C.J. Fombrun, N.M. Tichy, MA Devanna, 1984.

Strategic Human Resource Management: Theory and Practice by Graeme Salaman, John Storey, Jon Billsberry. Models of HRM (see, for example, Beer *et al.*, 1985; Guest, 1987).

Strategies to Retain Human Capital in Business Process Outsourcing (BPO) Industry, R. Raman, kohinoorgroup.co.in.

Systems Approach to Retention of Critical Employees, Kushal Vohra Sr—papers.ssrn.com.

The Significance of Human Resource Management: A reconsideration of the evidence—PF Boxall—Management: Critical Perspectives on Business and Management, 1999.

Understanding Human Resource Management in the Context of Organizations and their Environments—S.E. Jackson, R.S. Schuler—*Annual Reviews in Psychology*, 1995.

**10**

# Asset Liability Management
## Issues and Trends

SHEBA SANGEETHA

## ABSTRACT

With the increasing levels of globalization of the Indian Banking industry and the evolution of universal banks, competition in the Banking industry will intensify further. Strong capital positions and balance sheets place banks in a better position to deal with and absorb the economic shocks. Asset liability management is the practice of managing risks that arise due to mismatches between the assets and liabilities (debts and assets) of the bank. Banks face several risks such as liquidity risk, interest rate risk, credit risk and operational risk. Asset Liability Management (ALM) is a strategic management tool to manage interest rate risk and liquidity risk faced by banks, other financial services companies and corporations. Banks manage the risks of Asset liability mismatch by matching the assets and liabilities according to the maturity pattern or matching the duration by hedging and by securitization. This paper discusses issues in asset-liability management and elaborates on various categories of risks that are required to be managed. It examines strategies for asset-liability management from the asset side as well as the liability side, particularly in the Indian context.

## INTRODUCTION

With liberalisation in the Indian financial markets over the last few years and growing integration of domestic markets with external markets, the risks associated with banks' operations have become complex and large, requiring strategic management. Banks are now operating in a fairly deregulated environment and are required to determine on their own, interest rates on deposits and advance, in both domestic and foreign currencies on a dynamic basis. The interest rates on banks' investments in government and other securities are now market-related. Intense competition for business involving both the assets and liabilities, together with increasing volatility in the domestic interest rates as well as foreign exchange rates, has brought pressure on the management of banks to maintain a good balance among spreads, profitability and long-term viability. Imprudent liquidity management can put banks' earnings and reputation at great risk. These pressures call for structured and comprehensive measures and not just *ad hoc* action. The Management of banks has to base their business decisions on a dynamic and integrated risk management system and process, driven by corporate strategy. Banks are exposed to several major risks in the course of their business—credit risk, interest rate risk, foreign exchange risk, equity/ commodity price risk, liquidity risk and operational risk. It is, therefore, important that banks introduce effective risk management systems that address the issues related to interest rate, currency and liquidity risks.

Banks need to address these risks in a structured manner by upgrading their risk management and adopting more comprehensive Asset-Liability Management (ALM) practices. ALM, among other functions, is also concerned with risk management and provides a comprehensive and dynamic framework for measuring, monitoring and managing liquidity, interest rate, foreign exchange, equity and commodity price risks of a bank that needs to be closely integrated with the banks' business strategy. It involves assessment of various types of risks and altering the asset-liability portfolio in a dynamic way in order to manage risks.

## WHAT IS ALM?

*Asset-Liability Management* is active management of a bank's balance sheet to maintain a mix of loans and deposits consistent with its goals for long-term growth and risk management. Banks, in the normal course of business, assume financial risk by making loans at interest rates that differ from rates paid on deposits. Deposits often have shorter maturities than loans and adjust to current market rates faster than loans. The result is a balance sheet mismatch between assets (loans) and liabilities (deposits). The function of asset-liability management is to measure and control three levels of financial risk: interest rate risk (the pricing difference between loans and deposits), credit risk (the probability of default), and liquidity risk (occurring when loans and deposits have different maturities).

## HISTORY OF ALM

Historically, ALM has evolved from the early practice of managing liquidity on the bank's asset side, to a later shift to the liability side, termed liability management, to a still later realization of using both the assets as well as liabilities sides of the balance sheet to achieve optimum resources management. But that was till the 1970s. In the 1980s, volatility of interest rates in USA and Europe caused the focus to broaden to include the issue of interest rate risk. ALM's history can clearly be attributed to its long tradition in the banking sector.

- **1854**: The golden rule of banking coined by Otto Hübner (assets and liabilities should not have mismatched maturities).
- **1857**: The deposit base theory (*Bodensatztheorie*) developed by Adolph Wagner (difference between the maturity and termination of a deposit).

- **1879**: The realisation theory of Carl Knies (use of marketable assets to settle outstanding liabilities), which is referred to nowadays mostly as the "Shiftability Theory" according to Moulton (1918).

Traditionally, banks and insurance companies used accrual accounting for all their assets and liabilities. They would take on liabilities, such as deposits, life insurance policies or annuities. They would invest the proceeds from these liabilities in assets such as loans, bonds or real estate. All assets and liabilities were held at book value. Doing so, disguised the possible risks arising from how the assets and liabilities were structured.

Prior to the 1970's, such mismatches tended not to be a significant problem. Interest rates in developed countries experienced only modest fluctuations, so losses due to asset-liability mismatches were small or trivial. Many firms intentionally mismatched their balance sheets. Because yield curves were generally upward sloping, banks could earn a spread by borrowing short and lending long. Things started to change in the 1970s, which ushered in a period of volatile interest rates that continued into the early 1980s. Managers of many firms, who were accustomed to thinking in terms of accrual accounting, were slow to recognize the emerging risk. Increasingly, managers of financial firms focused on asset-liability risk. The problem was not that the value of assets might fall or that the value of liabilities might rise. It was that capital might be depleted by narrowing of the difference between assets and liabilities—that the values of assets and liabilities might fail to move in tandem. Asset-liability risk is a leveraged form of risk. Accrual accounting could disguise the problem by deferring losses into the future, but it could not solve the problem. Firms responded by forming asset-liability management (ALM) departments to assess asset-liability risk. They established ALM committees comprised of senior managers to address the risk.

Despite the longstanding tradition of ALM, adequately putting it into practice and finding the right methods continued to present challenges. The recent sub-prime crisis has shown that, even after 150 years, ALM is still in need of further development.

**Objectives of ALM**

Ever since the initiation of the process of deregulation of the Indian banking system and gradual freeing of interest rates to market forces, and consequent injection of a dose of competition among the banks, introduction of asset-liability management (ALM) in the public sector banks (PSBs) has been suggested by several experts. But, initiatives in this respect, on the part of most bank managements have been absent. The primary objective in asset-liability management is managing Net Interest Margin (NIM) , that is, the net difference between interest earning assets (loans) and interest paying liabilities (deposits) to produce consistent growth in the loan portfolio and shareholder earnings, regardless of short-term movement in interest rates. The objective of a good Asset Liability Management system is liquidity risk management and interest rate risk management. Profitability and long-term viability of the institution are also the main objectives of ALM, subject to the constraints of credit quality, liquidity and capital requirements.

## DIFFERENT APPROACHES TO ASSET LIABILITY ANALYSIS

Techniques for assessing asset-liability risk came to include gap analysis and duration analysis. These facilitated techniques of gap management and duration matching of assets and liabilities. Both approaches work well if assets and liabilities comprised fixed cash flows. Options, such as those embedded in mortgages or callable debt, posed problems that gap analysis could not address. Duration analysis could address these in theory, but implementing sufficiently sophisticated duration measures was problematic. Accordingly, banks and insurance companies also performed scenario analysis.

The traditional analysis aims to measure the rate sensitivity of the banks' liabilities while the duration gap analyses the price sensitivity. While rate sensitivity is the ability to re-price the principal on the asset or liability, price sensitivity denotes the extent to which the price of the asset and liability will change or move, with respect to the change in the interest rate. An asset or liability is normally classified as rate sensitive if :

- within the time interval under consideration, there is a cash flow;
- the interest rate resets/re-prices contractually during the interval;
- RBI changes the interest rates in cases where interest rates are administered; and
- it is contractually pre-payable or withdrawable before the stated maturities.

With the sophisticated approach, the bank will be in a position to assess the economic value changes to the market interest rates. The duration method acknowledges the time value of money and compares the price sensitivity of the assets with that of the liabilities to the market value of assets and liabilities. In addition, it also provides a comprehensive measure of interest rate risk for the banks' entire portfolio of assets and liabilities.

## RISK MEASUREMENT TECHNIQUES

There are various techniques for measuring exposure of banks to interest rate risks.

*Gap analysis model* : This model looks at the re-pricing gap that exists between the interest revenue earned on the bank's assets and the interest paid on its liabilities over a particular period of time. It highlights the net interest income exposure of the bank, to changes in interest rates in different maturity buckets. Re-pricing gaps are calculated for assets and liabilities of differing maturities. A positive gap indicates that assets get re-priced before liabilities, whereas, a negative gap indicates that liabilities get re-priced before assets. The basic weakness with this model is that this method takes into account only the book value of assets and liabilities and hence ignores their market value. This method therefore is only a partial measure of the true interest rate exposure of a bank. Gaps may be identified in the following time buckets:

- upto 1 month
- Over one month and upto 3 months
- Over 3 months and upto 6 months
- Over 6 months and upto 12 months
- Over 1 year and upto 3 years
- Over 3 years and upto 5 years
- Over 5 years
- Non-sensitive

The Gap is the difference between Rate Sensitive Assets (RSA) and Rate Sensitive Liabilities (RSL) for each time bucket. The positive Gap indicates that it has more RSAs than RSLs whereas the negative Gap indicates that it has more RSLs. The Gap reports indicate whether the institution is in a position to benefit from rising interest rates by having a positive Gap (RSA > RSL) or whether it is in a position to benefit from declining interest rates by a negative Gap (RSL > RSA). The Gap can, therefore, be used as a measure of interest rate sensitivity. Each bank should set prudential limits on individual Gaps with the approval of the Board/Management Committee. The prudential limits should have a bearing on the total assets, earning assets or equity. The banks may work out earnings at risk, based on their views on interest rate movements and fix a prudent level with the approval of the Board/Management Committee.

**Financing of Gap**

In case the negative gap exceeds the prudential limit of 20% of outflows, the bank may show by way of a foot note as to how it proposes to finance the gap to bring the mismatch within the prescribed limits. The gap can be financed from market borrowings.

*Duration model* : Duration is an important measure of the interest rate sensitivity of assets and liabilities as it takes into account the time of arrival of cash flows and the maturity of assets and liabilities. It is the weighted average time to maturity of all the preset values of cash flows. The larger the value of the duration, the more sensitive is the price of that asset or liability to changes in interest rates. A higher duration gap will result in greater degree of changes in market value of equity. A banking institution may create a duration gap to improve market value of equity depending on its interest rate view.

*Value at Risk:* Refers to the maximum expected loss that a bank can suffer over a target horizon, given a certain confidence interval. It enables the calculation of market risk of a portfolio for which no historical data exists. It is used extensively for measuring the market risk of a portfolio's assets and liabilities.

*Simulation :* Simulation models help to introduce a dynamic element in the analysis of interest rate risk. Gap analysis and duration analysis suffer from their inability to move beyond the static analysis of current interest rate risk exposures. Basically simulation models utilize computer power to provide *what if* scenarios. They alsc prepare scenario analysis with different degrees of rollovers and different level of asset securitization, asset sale and other realizations to evolve the contingency funding requirement.

## Asset-liability Management Strategies for Correcting Mismatch

The strategies that can be employed for correcting the mismatch can be either liability or asset driven. Asset driven strategies for correcting the mismatch focuses on shortening the duration of the asset portfolio. The commonly employed asset-based financing strategy is securitization.

Liability-driven strategies basically focus on lengthening the maturity profiles of liabilities. Such strategies can include for instance, issue of external equity in the form of additional equity shares or compulsorily convertible preference shares (which can also help in augmenting the Tier I capital of finance companies), issue of redeemable preference shares, subordinated debt instruments, etc.

Banks are in the business of maturity transformation. They accept deposits of varying maturity from customers and pay loans of different maturities on the other side. Apart from maturity transformation, banks also transfer the risk appetite of customers. They accept fixed rate deposits and give floating rate loans. Similarly, they accept floating rate deposits and pay fixed rate loans. All these activities result in concentration of liquidity and interest rate risk in a bank's book. Bankers have been managing these risks since the evolution of banking. It is only in the recent past that the complexities of liquidity and interest rate risk management have increased.

*Liquidity risk management* : Importance of liquidity risk management has been highlighted by Basel Committee on Banking Supervision in the document "Sound Practices of Managing Liquidity in Banking Organizations". World-wide banking regulators are mandating banks to conduct stress test and scenario analysis of liquidity risk and prepare contingency plans to meet liquidity requirements in unforeseen circumstances. Liquidity risk is measured through either stock approach or flow approach. Under stock approach, certain standard ratios are computed. Some of the ratios widely used in banks are Liquid assets to short-term liabilities, Core assets to core liabilities, Inter-bank borrowings to total assets, Overnight borrowings to total assets, etc. Under flow approach, cash flows are segregated into different maturity ladders and net funding requirement for a given time horizon is estimated. The net funding requirement over a given time horizon gives a fair idea of liquidity risk faced by an institution. Reserve Bank of India has prescribed some statutory returns for submission of data on liquidity risk and interest rate risk by banks. Generally banks perform an in-depth analysis of their liquidity profile analyzing:

- The profile of liability holders,
- The extent of purchased fund providers, and
- ABC analysis of depositors etc.

The Statement of Structural Liquidity may be prepared by placing all cash inflows and outflows in the maturity ladder according to the expected timing of cash flows. A maturing liability will be a cash outflow while a maturing asset will be a cash inflow.

*Interest rate risk management* : The phased deregulation of interest rates and the operational flexibility given to banks in pricing most of the assets and liabilities have exposed the banking system to Interest Rate Risk. Interest rate risk management in banking book is a major objective of any ALM system. Typically, a bank positions its assets and liabilities into trading book and banking book. Interest rate movements cause price changes in trading book and earnings/economic value changes in banking book. While trading book assets and liabilities are held to take advantage of short-term price movements, banking book assets and liabilities arise out of relationship/regulatory requirements and provide accrual income to a bank.

*Gap or mismatch risk :* A gap or mismatch risk arises from holding assets and liabilities and off-balance sheet items with different principal amounts, maturity dates or re-pricing dates, thereby creating exposure to unexpected changes in the level of market interest rates.

*Basis Risk :* Basis risk arises due to changes in market rates on different financial instruments by varying degree. The risk that the interest rate of different assets, liabilities and off-balance sheet items may change in different magnitudes is termed as basis risk.

*Embedded Option Risk :* Embedded option means possibility of alteration of cash flows. The depositors enjoy freedom to close their deposits at any time by paying penalty. Similarly, there are embedded options with loan products such as cash credit, demand loans and term loans.

*Price Risk :* Banks are required to mark to market their investment portfolio in, held for trading and available for sale category. In the financial markets, prices of instruments and yields are inversely related. As per Reserve Bank of India's guidelines banks may classify their investments into three categories viz. (a) Held for Trading (HFT) (b) Available for Sale (AFS) ,and (c) Held till Maturity (HTM). While securities in HFT and AFS categories are required to be marked to marked, the securities in HTM are not.

*Currency Risk:* Floating exchange rate arrangement has brought in its wake pronounced volatility adding a new dimension to the risk profile of banks' balance sheets. The increased capital flows across free economies following deregulation have contributed to increase in the volume of transactions. Large cross border flows together with the volatility has rendered the banks' balance sheets vulnerable to exchange rate movements. The simplest way to avoid currency risk is to ensure that mismatches, if any, are reduced to zero or near zero. Ever since the RBI (Exchange Control Department) introduced the concept of end of the day near square position in 1978, banks have been setting up overnight limits and selectively undertaking active day time trading. Following the introduction of "Guidelines for Internal Control over Foreign Exchange Business" in 1981, maturity mismatches (gaps) are also subject to control. Presently, banks are also free to set gap limits with RBI's approval but are required to adopt Value at Risk (VaR) approach to measure the risk associated with forward exposures. Thus the open position limits together with the gap limits form the risk management approach to forex operations. For monitoring such risks banks should follow the instructions contained in Circular A.D (M.A. Series) No. 52 dated December 27, 1997 issued by the Exchange Control Department.

### The Asset-Liability Committee (ALCO)

The scope of ALM activities has widened. Today, ALM departments are addressing (non-trading) foreign exchange risks and other risks. ALM has also been extended to non-financial firms. The Asset Liability Management (ALM) team is responsible for allocating funding to various lending products, and for ensuring that the currency, interest rate and maturity sensitivity characteristics of the Bank's assets and liabilities are within prescribed risk parameters. To achieve this, ALM makes extensive use of derivative instruments including currency swaps, interest rate swaps and other interest rate management products.

The Asset-Liability Committee (ALCO) should be responsible for ensuring adherence to the limits set by the Board as well as for deciding the business strategy of the bank (on the assets and liabilities sides) in line with the bank's budget and decided risk management objectives. The ALM Support Groups consisting of operating staff should be responsible for analysing, monitoring and reporting the risk profiles to the ALCO. The ALCO would also articulate the current interest rate view of the bank and base its decisions for future business strategy on this view. Keeping in view the level of computerisation and the current MIS in banks, adoption of a uniform ALM System for all banks may not be feasible. The final guidelines have been formulated to serve as a benchmark for those banks which lack a formal ALM System. Banks which have already adopted more sophisticated systems may continue their existing systems but they should ensure to fine-tune their current information and reporting system so as to be in line with the ALM System suggested in the Guidelines. The ALM team develops new products and innovative market solutions tailored to meet clients' individual hedging needs. As part of this, they collaborate with other units to provide technical training to borrowers on pricing, market execution and credit aspects of hedging products and participates in negotiations on Master Derivatives Agreements (MDAs) with borrowers. The ALM team works closely with clients to develop hedging strategies and market tools to achieve their specific debt management objectives. Broadly, there are 3 requirements to implement ALM in banks.

- Developing a better understanding of ALM concepts,
- Introducing an ALM information system, and
- Setting-up ALM decision-making processes (ALM Committee/ALCO).

## ALM Information Systems

ALM has to be supported by a management philosophy which clearly specifies the risk policies and tolerance limits. This framework needs to be built on sound methodology with necessary information system as back up. Information is the key to the ALM process. Considering the large network of branches and the lack of an adequate system to collect information required for ALM which analyses information on the basis of residual maturity and behavioural pattern it will take time for banks in the present state to get the requisite information. The problem of ALM needs to be addressed by following an ABC approach, i.e. analysing the behaviour of asset and liability products in the top branches accounting for significant business and then making rational assumptions about the way in which assets and liabilities would behave in other branches.

### Emerging Issues in the Indian Context

With the onset of liberalization, Indian banks are now more exposed to the vagaries of the international markets, than ever before because of the removal of restrictions, especially with respect to forex transactions. This makes it imperative to have proper asset-liability management systems in place. Asset-liability management becomes essential as it enables the bank to maintain its exposure to foreign currency fluctuations given the level of risk it can handle. An increasing proportion of investments by banks are being recorded on a marked-to-market basis and as such large portion of the investment portfolio is exposed to market risks. Countering the adverse impact of these changes is possible only through efficient asset-liability management techniques. As the focus on net interest margin has increased over the years, there is an increasing possibility that the risk arising out of exposure to interest rate volatility will be built into the capital adequacy norms specified by the regulatory authorities. This, in turn will require efficient asset-liability management practices.

## CONCLUSION

In a sense, ALM was a substitute for market-value accounting in the context of accrual accounting. It was a necessary substitute because many of the assets and liabilities of financial institutions could not—and still cannot—be marked to market. This spirit of market-value accounting was not a complete solution. A firm can earn significant mark-to-market profits but go bankrupt due to inadequate cash flow. Some techniques of ALM—such as duration analysis—do not address liquidity issues at all. Others are compatible with cash-flow analysis. With minimal modification, a gap analysis can be used for cash flow analysis. Today, financial firms are increasingly using market-value accounting for certain business lines. This is true of universal banks that have trading operations. For trading books, techniques of market risk management—value-at-risk (VaR), market risk limits, etc.—are more appropriate than techniques of ALM. In financial firms, ALM is associated with those assets and liabilities—those business lines—that are accounted for on an accrual basis.

The growth of OTC derivatives markets have facilitated a variety of hedging strategies. A significant development has been securitization, which allows firms to directly address asset-liability risk by removing assets or liabilities from their balance sheets. Banks should make sure that increased balance sheet size should not result in excessive asset liability mismatch resulting in volatility in earnings. There should be proper limit structures, which should be monitored by Asset Liability Management Committee (ALCO) on a regular basis. The effectiveness of ALM system should be improved with a good Fund Transfer Pricing system. New approaches that are referred to as liability driven investment ("LDI") solutions have also been introduced following recent changes in accounting standards and regulations that have led to an increased focus on liability risk management. LDI solutions advocate an approach to ALM that is expressed in terms of allocation to three building blocks (cash, liability-matching portfolio, and performance portfolio). Modern risk management now takes place from an integrated approach to enterprise risk management that reflects the fact that interest rate risk, credit risk, market risk, and liquidity risk are all interrelated.

## References

Fabozzi, F.J. and Konishi, A. (1995), Asset Liability Management. New Delhi : S. Chand & Co.

Jain, J.L. (1996), Strategic Planning for Asset Liability Management, *The Journal of the Indian Institute of Bankers*, 67(4).

Reserve Bank of India Weekly Statistical Supplements, Basic Statistical Returns, Annual Reports—'ALM and Risk Management Guidelines' http://bankingtides.blogspot.com/ Prof. Vijaya Raghavan R.

Noël Amenc Ph.D., Lionel Martellini Ph.D. and Volker Ziemann, An EDHEC Risk and Asset Management Research Centre Publication.

Pramod Vaidya and Arvind Shahi. Asset Liability Management in Indian Banks.

Basel Principles for the Management and Supervision of Interest Rate Risk.

Sound Practices for Managing Liquidity in Banking Organisations, February 2000.

R. Vaidyanathan, 'ALM—Trends in Indian Context', *ASCI Journal of Management*, 29(1), 39-48.

S. Scott MacDonald/Timothy, W. Koch, Management of Banking, New Delhi : Thomson Learning.

'Stress Testing for Interest Rate Risk Management', Ashish Srivastava Professional Banker, Dec. 2007.

# 11

# Indian Retail Banking Industry
## An Analysis

RANA ZEHRA MASOOD

All over the world, retail banking is of prime importance and particularly in recent years, it is gaining focus in India due to various factors including changing landscape of competition, regulatory environment, innovative technology, and evolving macroeconomic environment, numerous micro level demand and supply side factors and financial market reforms.

With the increasing levels of Globalization, Liberalization, Privatization and new reforms of the Indian banking sector, competition will become stiffer. Therefore, the banks who understand the market dynamics, identify intimidation, predict instability, show high degree of professionalism and enthusiasm in their implementation and cater promptly to the market needs will survive and prosper.

Retail banking in India is not a new phenomenon as India has experienced exponential growth in the field of retail banking. For the last few years it has become identical with conventional banking for many banks. The housing sector is undergoing a boom in its credit. The retail loan market has detrimentally undergone a change from the sellers' market to the buyers' market. The time is no more the same, when it was difficult to get loans from the bank. The services of retail banking are a group of financial services that include instalment loans, housing mortgages, equity credit loans, deposit services, and individual retirement accounts. This indicates that the retail loan market has shown unique growth and development over recent years.

In India, economic sector reforms of which banking sector reforms constituted an essential part, stressed liberalization of markets, privatization of ownership and globalization of the economy. These reforms led to a heightened consciousness of ownership and capital structure, improved competition, increased sovereignty, technological upgradation and performance change reflected in broad indicators of net worth, Net NPA/Net Advances Ratio, Return on Assets (RoA) and Capital to Risk Weighted Asset Ratio (CRAR).

The growth of the retail financial services sector has been a key development on the market front. Indian banks (both public and private) have not only been keen to tap the domestic market but also to compete in the global market place. New overseas banks have been equally keen to gain grip in the Indian market.

In comparison with wholesale banking or corporate banking, retail banking is a high sized business with many service providers competing for market share. Some retail banking services, for example, financial institutions, among the most profitable services offer credit cards, Consumer Credit, Financial Supermarket and Installation Credit. Retail banking refers to banking in which banking institutions execute transactions directly with consumers, rather than corporations or other banks.

Retail banking in a recent book has been described as "hotter than vandal" considering the fact that vindaloo, the Indian-English innovative curry available in umpteen number of restaurants of London, is indeed very hot and spicy, it seems that retail banking is supposed to be the in-thing in today's world of banking.

Unlike wholesale banking, retail banking focuses strictly on consumer markets. It refers to banking in which banking institutions execute transactions directly with consumers, rather than corporations or other banks and is quite broad in nature, as it refers to the dealing of commercial banks with individual customers, both on liabilities and assets sides of the balance sheet. Fixed, current/savings accounts on the liabilities side; and mortgages, loans (e.g., personal, housing, auto, and educational) on the assets side, are the more important of the products offered by banks. Related ancillary services include credit cards, or depository services. Retail banking entities provide a wide range of personal banking services which include: savings and checking accounts, mortgages, personal loans, bill paying services, as well as debit and credit cards, education loans, housing loans, term deposits, consumer durable loans, auto loans, insurance, on line banking. Although retail banking is, for the most part, mass-market determined, many retail banking products may also extend to small and medium sized businesses. Nowadays much of retail banking is streamlined electronically via Automated Teller Machines (ATMs), or through virtual retail banking known as online banking.

Retail banking sector today is characterized by three basic characteristics, which include:

- Numerous products (deposits, credit cards, insurance, investments and securities).
- Numerous channels of distribution (call center, branch, Internet and kiosk).
- Numerous customer groups (user, small business, and corporate).

Retail Banking has been a striking innovation in the commercial banking sector, as Globalization has brought ferocious competition from worldwide banks. In order to compete with new entrants efficiently commercial banks need to hold strong balance sheets, which specify the real strength of the bank. The entry of new private sector banks and foreign banks equipped with latest technology and technology-driven product lines have really sensitized the ordinary customers of the banking services to the need for quality in terms of innovative products as well as delivery process. These banks are forcefully targeting the retail business and as a result grabbing the market share of public sector banks. For public sector banks, a major budge in business policy to focus on retail may be best possible for the long-term from a returns/ risk point of view—provided they can create and improve infrastructure in terms of technology, people, processes and pricing. Essential reasons for support of retail growth are :

- Financial affluence and the subsequent increase in purchasing power have given an incentive to a consumer boom.
- Changing consumer demographics indicate immense potential for growth in consumption both qualitatively and quantitatively.
- Scientific factors played a key role. Pragmatism banking in the form of debit cards, Internet and phone banking, anywhere and anytime banking has attracted many new customers into the banking field. Technological innovations relating to increasing use of credit/debit cards, ATMs, direct debits and phone banking has contributed to the growth of retail banking in India.
- The earnings of the banks, which had strengthened the bottom lines of banks for the past few years, have been turn downward during the last two years. In such a scenario, retail business provides a good vehicle of profit maximization. Considering the fact that retail's share in impaired assets is far lower than the overall bank loans and advances, retail loans have put relatively less provisioning burden on banks apart from diversifying their income streams.
- Decline in interest rates has also contributed to the development of retail credit by generating demand for such credit.

If the processes and technology can be harnessed, retail banking could provide an ideal combination of higher margin businesses (such as credit cards, personal loans) as well as a fair degree of risk diversification on the entire portfolio. Indian retail banking offers incredible opportunities and is a booming sector in India.

- Marketing issues may be the key focus for the Global players entering in Indian market because of the nature of Indian retail banking market requires new entrant to have to devise marketing programs to establish and enhance brand awareness, which in turn will help the new entrant to show its presence and help to create a niche for them.
- India's retail-banking assets size is expected to grow at the rate of 18% till the next year (2009-10).
- Retail credit to drive the growth of retail banking in future.

At the present time banks, especially the public sector banks are coming out with innovative products and services at a regular pace. The problem is that while preparing a new product or service they are not taking into account the customers' requirements and timing to launch the product/ service. It is high time that they prepare strategies, which suit customers and delivery channels.

Apart from the current deposits, percentages of all other types of deposits declined during this period. Percentage of retail saving deposits to total savings deposits decreased from 76% in 2000-01 to 72% in 2007-08. Further, percentage of retail term deposits declines by 13% during 2000-01 to 2007-08. Total deposits also declined by 7.8% during this period through total quantum of total deposits increased by Rs. 440164 crore. The entire commercial bank has been issuing the credit cards for their customer. Credit cards have the immense growing capacity in Metro cities of the nation.

One of the most major developments in Indian banking in the recent past has been the speedy growth of the retail loan portfolios of private sector commercial banks. The entry of new generation private sector banks has changed the entire

TABLE I

**Different Types of Retail Bank Deposits of Schedule Commercial Banks in India**

| *Year* | *Current Deposits* | | *Savings Deposits* | | *Term Deposits* | | *Total Deposits* | |
|---|---|---|---|---|---|---|---|---|
| | *Total* | % | *Total* | % | *Total* | % | *Total* | % |
| (1) | (2) | (3) | (4) | (5) | (6) | (7) | (8) | (9) |
| 2000-01 | 15283 | 21.00 | 86603 | 76.00 | 166686 | 51.80 | 268573 | 52.80 |
| 2001-02 | 17838 | 21.70 | 101043 | 73.10 | 195390 | 50.90 | 314271 | 52.00 |
| 2002-03 | 23140 | 23.30 | 130654 | 77.00 | 249707 | 53.40 | 403501 | 54.70 |
| 2003-04 | 27020 | 24.00 | 160004 | 79.20 | 299152 | 55.20 | 486175 | 57.00 |
| 2004-05 | 31772 | 25.60 | 179947 | 77.50 | 335805 | 54.20 | 547525 | 56.10 |
| 2005-06 | 32597 | 24.90 | 213368 | 79.40 | 385861 | 53.39 | 631826 | 56.20 |
| 2006-07 | 40465 | 26.50 | 248512 | 75.10 | 402317 | 48.30 | 691294 | 52.50 |
| 2007-08 | 51421 | 25.00 | 273513 | 72.00 | 383804 | 38.80 | 708737 | 45.00 |

*Note* : % indicates percentage of total respective deposits.

*Source* : Special Statistics on Banking, *EPW*, March 2008.

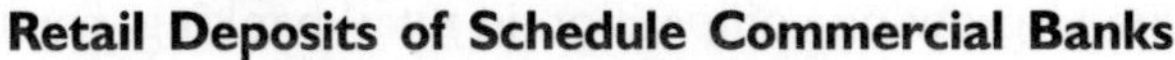


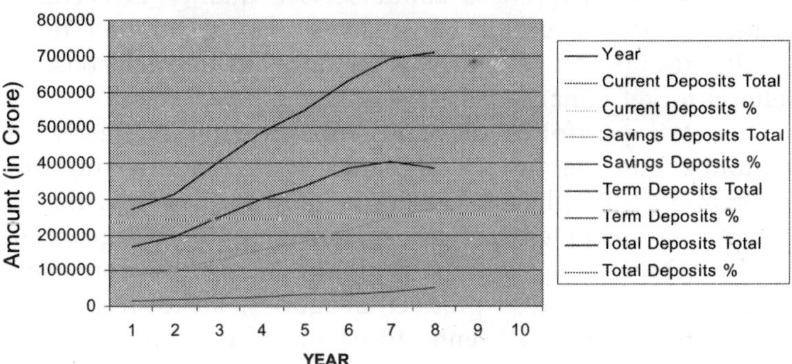


with the banks jumping over one another to provide elsewhere loans. The consumer has never been so lucky with so many banks offering so many products to choose from. With supply far exceeding demand it has been a competition to the bottom, with the banks undercutting one another. A lot of foreign banks have already burnt their fingers in the retail game and have now decided to get out of a few retail segments totally.

The private sector banks are posing a very stiff opposition to the public sector banks through their initiatives for meeting customer prospect and gaining a cutting edge. This is reflected by the growing market share and better profitability of private banks in comparison to that of public sector banks. The growth posted by some of the private sector banks has been such (a near doubling-up of retail credit in around two years which shows, yearly rate of growth of around 35 per cent) as to outperform the more modest attainments on this face by other banks—particularly the public sector banks. It has also created the awareness that overall financial situation have so changed that a major shift in business policy (such as the important focus on retail banking as against wholesale banking) is quite unsurprising and the prospect lies only in retail banking progress.

Due to growing competition in retail banking, considering the customer awareness about service quality is becoming essential. Public sector banks have also responded to the challenges posed by the private sector banks through conscious efforts to get enhanced their service quality.

Due to growing competition in retail banking, considering the customer awareness about service quality is becoming essential. Public sector banks have also responded to the challenges posed by the private sector banks through conscious efforts to get enhanced their service quality.

Retail portfolios of banks are growing by leaps and bounds, but the tie up of banks with dealers and their promotion through call centers is unluckily not giving due weight to customer care, thus, damaging the image of the banks. There is a need for exploring reasonable routes like brand building across product categories, takeover from the dealer, reverse the call center focus, etc. Strong brand name of products not only provides a competitive edge, but also improves the long-term relationship with customers.

The nimble-footed new generation private sector banks have taken a lead on this front and the public sector banks are trying to catch up. Housing loan accounts for a major hunk of retail loan. The PSBs have been losing business to the private sector banks in this segment.

The distinctive products offered in the Indian retail-banking sector are housing loans, consumption loans for purchase of durables, auto loans, credit cards and educational loans. The loans are marketed under outstanding brand names to make a distinction of the products offered by different banks.

Since the Report on Trend and Progress of India 2003-04 has shown that the loan values of this retail lending typically ranges between Rs. 20,000 to Rs. 100 lakh. The loans are generally for duration of five to seven years with housing loans granted for a longer duration of 15 years. Credit card is another rapidly growing sub-segment of this product group.

In recent past retail lending has turned out to be a key profit driver for banks with retail portfolio constituting 21.5 per cent of total outstanding advances as on March 2004. The overall mutilation of the retail loan portfolio worked out much less then the Gross NPA ratio for the entire loan portfolio. Retail loans have been a prime driver of credit growth in recent years, witnessing a growth of over 40% in 2004-05 and 2005-06. As a percentage of gross advances, it increased from 22% in 2003-04 to 25.5% in 2005-06. The key retail loan

**Retails Portfolio of Banks**

| Item | Outstanding March End | | Percentage variation | |
|---|---|---|---|---|
| | 2007 | 2008 | 2006-07 | 2007-08 |
| 1. Housing Loans | 224481 | 252932 | 25.4 | 12.7 |
| 2. Consumer Durables | 7296 | 4802 | 63.2 | -34.2 |
| 3. Credit Card Receivables | 18317 | 27437 | 47.3 | 49.8 |
| 4. Auto Loan | 82562 | 87998 | 34.5 | 6.6 |
| 5. Other Personal Loan | 1,55,204 | 197879 | 31.1 | 27.5 |
| Total Retail Loans | 487860 | 571048 | 29.9 | 17.1 |
| Total Loan Adv. of SCBs | 1893775 | 2332490 | 28.5 | 23.2 |

Source : RBI, Publication on Operators and Performance of Comm. Banks.

**Percentage Variation**

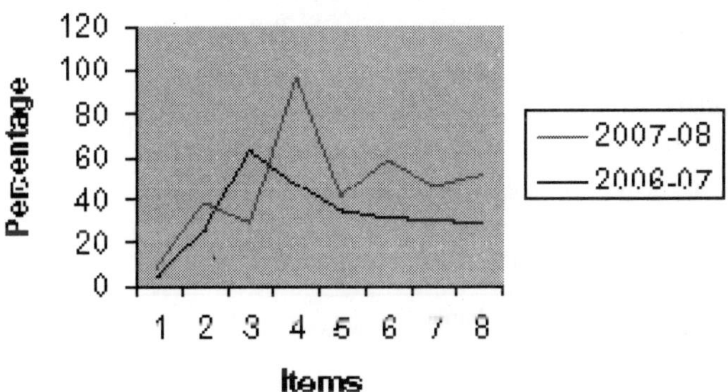


there has also been a growth in retail banking. However, even as the opportunities increase, there are some issues and challenges that Indian banks will have to contend with if they are to emerge successful in the medium to long-term.

For the period of 2006-07, gross credit extended by Indian commercial banks grew by 34.83% to touch INR 19, 495 billion. Retail credit constitutes about 25% of the total credit and has grown by 28.0% to INR 4,218.3 billion the annual growth in bank credit to the commercial sector is at 25.4% as on March 31, 2007 and was lower than 27.2% against previous year. Till

For the period of 2006-07, gross credit extended by Indian commercial banks grew by 34.83% to touch INR 19, 495 billion. Retail credit constitutes about 25% of the total credit and has grown by 28.0% to INR 4,218.3 billion the annual growth in bank credit to the commercial sector is at 25.4% as on March 31, 2007 and was lower than 27.2% against previous year. Till 2010, retail banking is likely to go up at a CAGR of 28% to touch a figure of INR9,700 billion. This requires expansion and diversification of retail product portfolio, better penetration and faster service mechanism.

## Deposit and Credit Growth

| | *As on Jan. 4, 2008* | *As on Jan. 2, 2009* |
|---|---|---|
| **DEPOSIT** | | |
| Public sector banks | 24.2 | 24.2 |
| Foreign banks | 34.1 | 12.1 |
| Private sector banks | 26.9 | 13.4 |
| Scheduled commercial banks* | 25.1 | 21.2 |
| **CREDIT** | | |
| Public sector banks | 19.8 | 28.6 |
| Foreign banks | 30.7 | 16.9 |
| Private sector banks | 24.2 | 11.8 |
| Scheduled commercial banks* | 21.4 | 24.0 |

*Includes regional rural banks

**BANKING SHARE**

| | *Public sector banks* | | | *Private banks* | | | *Foreign banks* | | |
|---|---|---|---|---|---|---|---|---|---|
| | *1998-99* | *2003-04* | *2007-08* | *1998-99* | *2003-04* | *2007-08* | *1998-99* | *2003-04* | *2007-08* |
| Deposits | 87.16 | 79.92 | 74.32 | 7.95 | 14.96 | 19.85 | 4.89 | 5.12 | 5.83 |
| Advances | 85.00 | 75.26 | 72.93 | 8.37 | 17.71 | 20.46 | 6.63 | 7.03 | 6.61 |
| Assets | 85.72 | 76.40 | 70.17 | 7.73 | 16.71 | 21.29 | 6.55 | 6.89 | 8.53 |
| Net Profit | 76.55 | 72.13 | 62.44 | 9.44 | 17.86 | 22.03 | 14.01 | 10.02 | 15.53 |

Retailing in fact makes ample business sense in the banking sector. In new era, private sector banks have been able to create a place in this regard; the public sector banks have not lagged behind. Leveraging their huge branch network and outreach, public sector banks have forcefully forayed to gather a larger portion of the retail tart. By international standards, however, there is still much scope for retail banking in India. After all, retail loans constitute less than seven per cent of GDP in India *vis-à-vis* about 35 per cent for other Asian economies—South Korea (55%), Taiwan (52%), Malaysia (33%) and Thailand (18%). Since retail banking in India is still mounting from self-effacing base, there is a possibility that the growth numbers seem to get somewhat overstated. One, therefore, has to work out caution is interpreting the growth of retail banking in India.

Retail banking is distinctive mass-market banking where individual customers use limited branches of larger commercial banks. Services offered include: savings and inspection of Retail banking on one hand offers development opportunities, it also offers challenges on the other hand. The development and success of the retail market (in the banking sector) will depend upon the aptitude and ability of the banks to meet with the challenges and make the best use of the opportunities.

The challenges in front of the Indian organized retail sector are many and these are stopping the Indian retail industry from attainment its full potential. The performance of the Indian consumer has been modified. This has happened for the Indian consumer is earning more now, western influences, and women working force is increasing, desire for luxury items and better quality. Customer now wants to consume, store, and get entertained under the same roof. All these have lead the Indian organized retail sector to give more in order to satisfy the Indian customer.

The biggest challenge facing the Indian organized retail sector is the lack of retail breathing space. With real estate prices increasing due to increase in demand from the Indian organized retail sector, it is posing a challenge to its growth.

With Indian retailers having to shell out more for retail space it is affecting their overall success in retail. Lack of skilled manpower is a challenge facing the organized retail sector in India. The Indian retailers have difficultly in finding trained person and also have to pay more in order to retain them. This again brings down the Indian retailers profit levels.

Customer maintenance is more demanding in India, these days it has in fact become tricky to keep hold of a client as the competition level has amplified so much in India, which not only have made procurer educated about banking but have made them more challenging for the services offered by a bank. They demand for services and if the bank is unable to serve them, it loses revenue around 0.25% from a stand alone customer which impact on its profit and assets on a large scale if unsatisfied number of customer is increased.

The banking industry today faces unprecedented challenges and increasing pressures to contain costs, realize economies of scale, and improve efficiencies. Our retail banking solutions emphasize standardization and measurability, providing efficient, cost-effective process handling while streamlining systems to maximize growth and drive revenue. In invigorating for tomorrow, the kind of expertise used and the effectiveness of operations would provide the much needed competitive edge for success in retail Banking Business. In addition:

- With retail customers demanding easier access to an array of ever more sophisticated financial products, banks need to manage complex data sets for individual customer accounts.
- New investment instruments, mortgages, lines of credit, small-business loans, and personal financial advisory services all require data quality, online account management, document production, and more secure archiving solutions.
- Mergers and acquisitions are fueling growth and increasing product portfolios, but require wide-

ranging data consolidation and integration efforts to realize promised economies of scale.

- Banks need to offer customers with faster and more complete statements in the mail as well as secure, immediate online entrée to current and past financial statements.
- Since shareholders demand higher margins, retail banks must continuously adjust their mix of services to accommodate speedily changing business conditions. Customer intelligence has become the key to identifying, acquiring and retaining high-margin account holders.

## References


Gopinath, S., "Retail Banking—Opportunities and Challenges", *RBI Bulletin*, LIX, No. 6, June (2005).

Divanna, J.A., "The Future of Retail banking", Palgrave Macmillan, New York, 2004.

EPW Research Foundation, Increasing Concentration of Banking Operations—Top Centres and Retail Loans", *EPW*, Vol. XLI, No. 11, March, 2008.

Dey, S. and Maji, S.G., "Need to Improve Customer Service in Banks: An Indian Perspective", *The Management Accountant*, Vol. 41, No. 12, December 2006.

Sudhir, M., "Retail Banking in India—The Paradigm Shift", *Chartered Financial Analyst*, Vol. XI, No. 2, December 2005.

Berger, A.N., W.C. Hunter, and S.G. Tamc (1993), "The Efficiency of Financial Institutions: A Review and Preview of Research Past, Present and Future", *Journal of Banking and Finance.*

Berger, A.N., A.K. Kashyap, and J.M. Scalise (1995), "The Transformation of the U.S. Banking Industry: What a Long, Strange Trip it's been", *Brookings Papers on Economic Activity*, 1995, New York, U.S.A.

Brynjolfsson, E. and L. Hit (1996), "Paradox Lost? Firm-level Evidence on the Returns to Information Systems Spending", *Management Science.*

Cates, D.C. (1991), "Can Bank Mergers Build Shareholder Value?", *Journal of Bank Accounting and Finance*, 1996, London, England.

Prasad, B. and P.T. Harker (1997), "Examining the Contribution of Information Technology Toward Productivity and Profitability in U.S. Retail Banking", *Working Paper 97-09*, Financial Institutions

Center, The Wharton School, University of Pennsylvania (Philadelphia, PA); available at http://wrdsenet.wharton.upenn.edu/fic/wfic/papers.html

Hunter, L.W. (1997), "Transforming Retail Banking: Inclusion and Segmentation in Service Work", Working Paper, Wharton Financial Institutions Center, The Wharton School (Philadelphia, PA).

RBI's Report on Trends and Progress in Indian Banking 2004.

Annual Policy of RBI 2004-05.

RBI's Publication on Operation and Performance of Commercial Banks (2007-08).

www.indiastat.com

www.rbi.org.in

12

# Non-resident Indians' Investment Opportunities in India

M. CHANDRASEKARAN AND M.K. DURGAMANI

Globalizing the economy, the Government of India has taken special care to get increasing involvement of non-resident Indian in the industrial development of the country. The government of India has offered a number of other facilities and incentives to non-resident Indians/persons of Indian orgin and overseas corporate bodies to enlist their greater participation in the economic development of the country.

## NON-RESIDENT INDIANS

Many Indian staying abroad many of them have taken the citizenship of that country, but they have their roots in India. Some non-residents of Indian nationality or person of Indian orgin residing abroad are often called "NRI". They are given many facilities in India without losing their status as foreign citizen.

## DEFINITION OF NRI

Foreign Exchange Regulations Act, 1973 (FERA) the definition of person resident outside India is based on the number of days stay in India during the course of preceding financial year.

Bank plays an important role in all Foreign Exchange Transactions in India. All receipts and payments of foreign exchange are required to be settled in almost all cases through a ban authorized to deal in foreign exchange. Sec. 10 of FEMA requires a ban to obtain a license from Reserve Bank of India (RBI) to deal in foreign exchange and such banks are the "Authorized Dealers" in foreign exchange.

Indian nationals and persons of Indian origin resident abroad can open bank accounts in India freely, out of funds remitted from abroad in foreign exchange, or out of funds legitimately due to them in India. RBI has granted general permission to "Authorized Dealers" (AD) to open such accounts.

There are various types of NRI account, they are : (i) Foreign currency Non-Resident (FCNR(B)), (ii) Non-Resident (Non-Reportable) Rupee Deposit Accounts (NR(NR)RD).

FCNR(B) Account is NRIs/PIOs/OCBs are permitted to open such accounts in US Dollars, Sterlin Punts, Deutsche marks, Japanese Yen and Euro. The account may be opened only in the form of term deposit for any of the three maturity periods viz. (a) one year and above but less than two years, (b) two years and above but less than three years, and (c) three years only.

Interest incomes of these deposits are tax free in the hands of NRI until he maintains a non-resident status or a resident but not ordinarily resident status under the Income tax laws.

FCNR(B) account can also be utilized for local disbursements including payment for exports from India, repatriation of funds abroad and for making investments in India, as per foreign investment guidelines

NR(E)RA accounts eligible to open NRIs, PIOs and OCBs. These are rupee dominated accounts. Accounts can be in the form of savings, current, recurring or fixed deposit accounts. These deposits can be used for all legitimate purposes. The balance in the account is freely reportable interest lying to the credit of NR(E)RA account is exempt from tax in the hands of the NRI.

NR(NR)RD account eligible to open NRIs/PIOs/OCB, other non-resident individuals/entities are permitted to open this accounts. This accounts can be opened by transfer of freely convertible foreign currency funds from abroad, or form NE(E)RA/FCNR accounts deposits can be held. Jointly with a resident. This deposit can be for period from 6 months to 3 years and can be renewed further.

## OBJECT OF THE STUDY

- To study the types of bank accounts available to NRIs in India,
- To study investment opportunities available to NRIs in India, and
- To provide suggestions for better utilization of investment opportunities of NRIs in India and improving deposit levels in India

## METHODOLOGY OF THE STUDY

This study is completely based on secondary data. The required secondary data were collected from various libraries, RBI bulletins, World Bank Report, Published Journal and website.

## RESEARCH HYPOTHESIS

There is no significant relationship between Direct Investment and NRI.

## FRAMEWORK OF ANALYSIS

The researcher has applied the following statistical tools

for analyzing the data and drawing inferences. They are t-test, correlation, least square trend analyses

TABLE I

**Actual and Trend Value of FCNR (B)**

*(US $ Million)*

| *X* Year | *Y* FCNR (B) Actual value | *Trend value* |
|---|---|---|
| 1998 | 8467 | 7153 |
| 1999 | 7835 | 7876 |
| 2000 | 8172 | 8598 |
| 2001 | 9076 | 9319 |
| 2002 | 9673 | 10042 |
| 2003 | 10199 | 10764 |
| 2004 | 10961 | 11486 |
| 2005 | 11452 | 12208 |
| 2006 | 13064 | 12930 |
| 2007 | 15129 | 13652 |
| | 104028 | 104028 |

*Source* : RBI Bulleting.

Y 2008 = 14374
Y 2009 = 15096
Y 2010 = 15818
Y 2011 = 16540
Y 2012 = 17262

From Table 1 it is clear that the total FCNR(B) funds are continuously increased year after year except in the year 1999. the trend value of this scheme is increased year by year. The trend value is US $ 7153 million in year 1998 but it is increased to US$ 17262 million in 2012.

TABLE 2

**Actual Trend Value of NR(E) RA**

(*US $ Million*)

| *X* *Year* | *Y* *NR(E)RA Actual value* | *Trend value* |
|---|---|---|
| 1998 | 5637 | 2794 |
| 1999 | 6045 | 5226 |
| 2000 | 6758 | 7659 |
| 2001 | 7147 | 10089 |
| 2002 | 8449 | 12521 |
| 2003 | 14923 | 14953 |
| 2004 | 20559 | 17385 |
| 2005 | 21291 | 19817 |
| 2006 | 22070 | 22249 |
| 2007 | 24495 | 24681 |
| | 137374 | 137374 |

*Source* : RBI Bulleting.

Y 2008 = 27113
Y 2009 = 29545
Y 2010 = 31976
Y 2011 = 34408
Y 2012 = 36840

The projected trend for the future period the values are increasing nature. The projected trend value at the year of 2012 at US $ 36840 millions.

Table 3 analyzed that the actual increased up to 2002 after that it is in a diminishing trend. The trend value of this scheme was decline nature year after year during the entire study period. The highest actual value of US $ 7052 million on 2002 and the lowest value US $ 232 million on 2005. The highest trend value of US $ 8099 million during 1998 and lowest trend value of this scheme was US $ -315 million during the year 2007.

TABLE 3

**Actual Trend Value of NR(NR) RD**

*(US $ Million)*

| X<br>*Year* | Y<br>*NR(NR)RD Actual value* | *Trend value* |
|---|---|---|
| 1998 | 6262 | 8099 |
| 1999 | 6618 | 7164 |
| 2000 | 6754 | 6229 |
| 2001 | 6849 | 5294 |
| 2002 | 7052 | 4359 |
| 2003 | 3407 | 3424 |
| 2004 | 1746 | 2490 |
| 2005 | 232 | 1555 |
| 2006 | — | 620 |
| 2007 | — | -315 |
| | 38920 | 38920 |

*Source* : RBI Bulleting.

## INVESTMENT OPPORTUNITIES FOR NON-RESIDENT INDIANS

Non-resident Indians' investment in viewed as complementary to the efforts of the people within India to steer the country towards economic development. In almost every country of the world one would come across persons of Indian origin. These persons of Indian origin abroad, known as "Overseas Indians" include:

(a) Foreign citizens of Indian origin who have adopted the nationality of the country of their residence.
(b) Indian citizens residing abroad who hold Indian passports and are known as "permanent" residents in a foreign country.
(c) Indian citizens holding Indian passports who are "temporary" residents in a foreign country.
(d) Persons of Indian origin who have become "state-

less" as neither do they have Indian citizenship or the citizenship of the country of their present residence.

In this analysis the FDI represent dependent variable and NRI represents independence variable.

TABLE 4

**Analysis of the Relationship between NRI and FDI**

*(US $ Million)*

| *X* <br> *NRI* | *Y* <br> *FDI* | $\overline{X}$ <br> *(X–X)* | $\overline{Y}$ <br> *(Y–Y)* | $X^2$ | $Y^2$ | *XY* |
|---|---|---|---|---|---|---|
| 241 | 3557 | 192.1 | -2542.4 | 36902.41 | 6463797.76 | -488395.04 |
| 62 | 2462 | 13.1 | -3637.4 | 171.61 | 13230678.76 | -47649.94 |
| 84 | 2155 | 35.1 | -3944.4 | 1232.01 | 15558291.36 | -138448.44 |
| 67 | 4029 | 18.1 | -2070.4 | 327.61 | 4286556.16 | -37474.24 |
| 35 | 6130 | -13.9 | 30.6 | 193.21 | 936.36 | -425.34 |
| — | 5035 | — | -1064.4 | — | 1132947.36 | — |
| — | 4322 | — | -1777.4 | — | 3159150.76 | — |
| — | 6051 | — | -48.4 | — | 2342.56 | — |
| — | 7722 | — | 1622.6 | — | 2632830.76 | — |
| — | 19531 | — | 13431.6 | — | 180407878.6 | — |
| 489 | 60994 | | | 38826.85 | 226875410.4 | -712393 |

*Source* : RBI Bulleting.

$$X = \frac{489}{10} = 48.9$$

$$Y = \frac{60994}{10} = 6099.4$$

$$r = \frac{\Sigma xy}{\sqrt{\Sigma x^2 \ \Sigma y^2}}$$

$$r = -0.240$$

Table 4 analyse the relationship of NRI and FDI is low degree of negative correlation. NRI and FDI are analysed by using t-test and the result is given below.

**Null Hypothesis**

There is no significant relationship between NRI and FDI.

$$t = \frac{r}{\sqrt{1-r^2}} \times \sqrt{n-2}$$

$$t = \frac{-0.240}{\sqrt{1-(-0.240)^2}} \times \sqrt{10-2}$$

$$t = -0.720$$

Degree of freedom = 8
Significance level = 5%
Table value of t = 2.306
Calculated value = -0.720

The calculated value is less than the table value. Hence the null hypothesis is accepted. So there is no significant relationship between NRI and FDI.

## SUGGESTIONS

- FCNR(B) AND NR(E)RA account trend for the future period the values are increasing nature. So government maintain the account.
- The inflows into NE(E)Ra deposits from 2002-03 on wards may partly be due to crediting of maturity proceeds of the NR(E)RA deposits from 2002-03 onwards may partly be due to crediting of maturity proceeds of the NR(NR)RD deposits which were discontinued with effect from April 1, 2002. The deposits in India Banking Institutions to offer many more attractive schemes related to NRI.

- The NRI investment in India are in negative trend, the government is to take necessary steps to improve their NRI deposits in India through Financial institutions.

## CONCLUSION

The researcher analyse the NRI investment opportunities in total FDI growth of NRI Deposits FCNR(B), NR(NR)RD and NR(E)RA accounts.

This type of study helps to asses the amount of deposits made by NRIs in Indian commercial banks and helps to forecast future dposits also. A research study on "NRI investment in India" may be undertaken by future researcher to assess investment made by NRIs in various sectors of Indian economy.

### REFERENCES

Chanchal Chopra, Foreign Investment in India, Deep & Deep Publications Pvt. Ltd.

Mayur Nayak, NRIs Investments, Taxations and FEMA, Show white Publications Pvt. Ltd.

RBI Bulletin.

# 13

# Internet Banking and its Challenges

S. Uma

## INTRODUCTION

Internet has touched almost all aspects of our lives. The emergence of e-commerce has revolutionized the way we live, shop, entertain and interact. Therefore, it should not come as a surprise if it tries to influence the way we save and the way we invest.

Today, when the customer is king and the service providers are rushing to pay obeisance to the king, financial service providers cannot be left behind. In their quest to differentiate their services and gain competitive advantage over their competitors, the financial service providers are trying to provide their services to the customers in the comfort of their homes. The Internet has emerged as a convenient channel for these service providers.

With cybercafés and kiosks springing up in different cities access to the Net is going to be easy. Internet banking (also referred as e-banking) is the latest in this series of technological wonders in the recent past involving use of Internet for delivery of banking products and services. Even the Morgan Stanley Dean Witter Internet research emphasized that Web is more important for retail financial services than for many other industries.

Internet banking is changing the banking industry and is having the major effects on banking relationships. Banking is now no longer confined to the branches were one has to approach the branch in person, to withdraw cash or deposit a cheque or request a statement of accounts. In true Internet banking, any inquiry or transaction is processed online without any reference to the branch (anywhere banking) at any time. Providing Internet banking is increasingly becoming a "need to have" than a "nice to have" service. The net banking, thus, now is more of a norm rather than an exception in many developed countries due to the fact that it is the cheapest way of providing banking services.

Living in India, we might find these ideas too far fetched but the truth is that Internet has changed the way these services are delivered, particularly in countries where the Internet penetration is high. The different ways in which Internet is trying to revolutionize the delivery of the financial services and products are given below:

1. Internet Banking
2. Electronic Bill Payment
3. Online Brokerages
4. Online Delivery of Financial Products like Mortgages

## 1. INTERNET BANKING

Two distinct trends can be discerned in the realm of Internet Banking. On one hand, Banks and Financial Institutions are trying to enter into new areas and consolidate their hold on the entire financial sector. On the other hand, new Dot Coms are entering the financing business and challenging the banks. It could be said that two opposite things are happening at the same time. The banks, via their consolidation moves are trying to preserve their strongholds, while the Dot Coms are trying to fragment the market by providing superior services. Banks and Financial Institutions are trying to leverage their Brands and their position in the industry. While, the Dot Coms are using their competency in superior service design and experience of competing in this highly unstable environment. All the players share the same objectives: acquiring customers, providing them with new financial information, services, and products, and doing so in a way that enhances the value proposition of their products and services.

Internet Banking allows the Banks (and other Financial Service providers) to overcome the tradeoff between content and reach. With the use of Internet, banks can provide their services to a much wider audience then they could do without it. Even before the coming of Internet, competition had shifted from products to services. This was due, in large part, to the advent of Private Sector Banks.

Before the entry of these banks, the retail banking was more of a commodity with hardly any differentiation on the basis of products or services. Banks offered similar products and similar service. But the new private sector banks changed the scenario by differentiating on the basis of service. They started providing Telephone based banking and introduced the concept of home banking. The superior service being provided by these banks was the main reason for their rapid growth. But their reach was limited due to logistics of setting up branches and increasing the reach of their service. Any attempt to increase the branch network would have increased their overheads and any attempt to widen the areas being served by a branch was likely to lead to deterioration in the service levels. In other words, these banks were caught in a dilemma as they faced the Reach and content tradeoff. With the advent of Internet these banks have been able to overcome this tradeoff.

By using the Internet, these banks can expand their reach as well as maintain the standards of their services.

## 2. ELECTRONIC BILL PAYMENT

From the point of view of Banks, Electronic Bill Payment (EBP) represents something of a threat, in that it could lead to customer attrition and reduce revenue. Among other revenue streams, the following sources of funds for the banks could be affected:

- Float associated with processing in the physical form,
- Cash Management Services.

The Banks can protect itself by providing this service to their customers. But EBP also has an important strategic dimension, as it can become an integral part of a bank's portfolio of services. EBP can attract customers to the bank by making transactions more efficient and enabling customers to access their financial information more easily. Moreover, online interactions allow use of such tools as e-CRM to create a more intimate relationship with the customer and promote and deliver other online products and services.

If the Banks do not establish control on EBP, they are likely to loose customers to the new providers of financial services, thus affecting other sources of revenue.

In India, HDFC Bank, ICICI Bank and Citibank are trying set-up an EBP portal. ICICI has already started a portal called BillJunction.com. Banks are planning to use the Net for payment of utility bills. They are entering into tie-ups with utilities like MTNL, Airtel, Orange, and BPL Mobile, etc. Right now, a customer who's received a bill in the physical form logs into the network in order to make an online payment. In the future, these bills will be sent to customers through the Net.

Consumers and Businesses can derive economic benefit on account of reduction in transaction costs and a reduction in the float resulting from physical processing of the Bills. In addition, many are likely to adopt it mainly for the convenience. They can pay bills electronically in the same way they do today, but by consolidating their bills, they can reduce the effort involved in the whole process. They can also access their account at the same time. They can conveniently access all billers from a single portal that also provides them banking facilities. This would enable them to view their account balance while paying bills. For portals or the intermediaries that consolidate bills from multiple billers at a single online location EBP is a tool to acquire customers and provide them other financial services also. Dominance of the EBP market can lead to an entry into other financial services markets such as credit or debit card payments, or indeed into a much broader range of e-commerce markets, such as payments gateways.

## 3. ONLINE BROKERAGE

Online Broking is emerging as another field where traditional service providers are likely to face tough competition from the Dot Coms. In Taiwan and Korea, 30% of the stock trading has already moved online. This is posing a threat to the traditional Full-Service Brokerages. By leveraging the power of the web, Charles Schwab has emerged as a major threat to Full-Service brokers like Merrill Lynch. In order to preempt the moves into these areas by new players, many Banks have already tied up with Online Brokerages.

The Banks have entered the e-trading business. Since many banks are also Depositary participants, they have tied up with e-traders so that a customer is able to buy or sell shares online and make and receive payments through the Net.

In India, HDFC Bank has tied up with Investsmart.com and is offering its services to all the clients of the brokerage. ICICI Bank has gone a step ahead and launched ICICIDirect.com. These banks have become exclusive providers of banking and depositary/custodial services to the clients of these online brokerages.

## 4. ONLINE DELIVERY OF FINANCIAL PRODUCTS

The Banks have started offering banking services like checking your account status fund transfer, ordering demand drafts and writing out cheques, via the net. Soon these will form only a small part of the total array of services being offered by them. These Banks have embarked on a number of new initiatives to protect their stronghold and to leverage the net. They are offering value-added services to their customers and at the same time are trying to get into B2C and B2B e-commerce. They are even trying to get their finger into various transactions between the Government on one side and the business and the customer on the other. Banks are trying to become a part of the online value chain. For example, they are trying to tie up with corporates so as to become a part of their supply chain and enable electronic transfer of funds between the different components of the Supply Chain. They are doing this by acting as an intermediary between the corporations and their vendors by enabling online transactions at one place.

Some Banks are trying to set-up portals for routing payments like Excise Duty and Sales Tax. Not content with that Banks are setting up secure payment gateways to tap the B2C online market.

Banks have taken the application process for personal loans, car loans, and mortgage, online. They plan to offer other financial products like Bonds and Mutual Funds through their financial service portal. This strategy is aimed by pre-empting the entry of new startups into this business.

Another bit of the Net strategy, involves providing infrastructure for B2C as well as B2B e-commerce. Banks are setting up secure payment gateways that will allow online retail shops to obtain instant credit card verifications. Once the buyer hits the pay button at a B2C portal, the buyer's credit card details will get encrypted and travel securely to the Visa or MasterCard approval system through the bank's payment gateway.

The banks are also setting up their own shopping portals. HDFC has a stake in a portal called easy2buy.com where HDFC bank customers can buy using their bank account number. Federal Bank has similar arrangements with Rediff.com and Fabmart.com. ICICI has set-up Magiccart.com, an e-tailing site.

At the B2B end, Banks are offering Net Banking service that allows electronic fund transfers among a company, its vendors and dealers. Another service being targeted at this segment is cash management. This will reduce the float, which is present in physical processing of the payments. The Banks are also trying to integrate their systems with the ERP/Supply Chain system of their clients. This will enable the bank to benefit from the movement towards e-procurement. E-Procurement involves making transactions online and processing the payment electronically.

## CHALLENGES

One of the challenges before a Bank, which is trying to become e-enabled is that the data is scattered across the countries. Integration of this data is necessary if the banks have to succeed on the net. The second challenge is related to the move towards expanding the basket of financial products being offered by Financial Service providers. In developed countries, Financial Service providers are using the Internet as a media for expanding into new products. Banks are getting into Mutual funds and *vice-versa*. However, in India, archaic regulations do not allow companies to have a close relationship with the Banks owned by them or to offer products, which are offered by another category of service providers. As a result, companies like ICICI are forced to keep their Banking arms separate from the main company. They are also prevented from offering products, which fall under the purview of Banks. This is a serious impediment for innovation in the financial service sector. Moreover, it prevents Indian Financial Service Providers from exploiting the power of the web.

## CONCLUSION

Given these challenges, only a Bank (or Financial Service provider) which moves fast and tries to capture the first mover advantage can think of succeeding in this sector. Another Key Success Factor will be the Value, which the online operations of the Banks will be offering to the consumer. This is what will differentiate between similar offerings from many providers of financial products and services. Starting now, will give the organization an advantage in terms of the networking it will be able to achieve. This will help it in meeting the first challenge. Banks (or Financial Service providers) should be ready to launch their operations within days of the liberalization of the sector. This will allow them to reach a critical mass and establish themselves in the e-World.

# *Mobile Banking*

## *Trends and Challenges*

S. Uma, V. Sridevi and K. Sumathi

### MEANING

Mobile banking (also known as M-Banking, m-banking, SMS Banking, etc.) is a term used for performing balance checks, account transactions, payments, etc. via a mobile device such as a Mobile Phone. To avail this service one has to open an account with the Bank that provides this Mobile Banking facility and register for Mobile Banking Serives.

### A MOBILE BANKING CONCEPTUAL MODEL

In one academic model[1] mobile banking is defined as:

"Mobile Banking refers to provision and availment of banking—and financial services with the help of mobile telecommunication devices. The scope of offered services may include facilities to conduct bank and stock market transactions, to administer accounts and to access customised information."

## TRENDS IN MOBILE BANKING

The ability to offer Financial transaction online has also created new players in the financial services industry, such as online banks, online brokers and wealth managers who offer personalized services, although such players still account for a tiny percentage of the industry.

Over the last few years, the mobile and wireless market has been one of the fastest growing markets in the world and it is still growing at a rapid pace. According to a study by financial consultancy celent 35% of online banking households will be using mobile banking by 2010, up from less than 1% today. Upwards of 70% of bank center call volume is projected to come from mobile phones. Mobile banking will eventually allow users to make payments at the physical point of sale. "Mobile contact less payment" make up 10% of the contactless market by 2010.[2]

Many believe that mobile users have just started to fully utilize the data capabilities in their mobile phones. In Asian countries like India, China and Phillipines, where mobile infrastructure is comparatively better than the fixed-line infrastructure, and in European countries, where mobile phone penetration is very high (at least 80% of consumers use a mobile phone), mobile banking is likely to appeal even more.

This opens up huge markets for financial institutions interested in offering value-added services. With mobile technology, banks can offer a wide range of services to their customers such as doing funds transfer while travelling, receiving online updates of stock price or even performing stock trading while being stuck in traffic. According to the German mobile operator Mobilcom, mobile banking will be the "killer application" for the next generation of mobile technology.

Mobile devices, especially smartphones, are the most promising way to reach the masses and to create "stickiness" among current customers, due to their ability to provide services anytime, anywhere, high rate of penetration and potential to grow. According to Gartner shipment of smartphones is growing fast, and should top 20 million units (of over 800 million sold) in 2006 alone.

In the last 4 years, banks across the globe have invested billions of dollars to build sophisticated internet banking capabilities. As the trend is shifting to mobile banking, there is a challenge for CIOs and CTOs of these banks to decide on how to leverage their investment in internet banking and offer mobile banking, in the shortest possible time.

## MOBILE BANKING SERVICES

Mobile banking can offer services such as the following:

### Account Information

1. Mini-statements and checking of account history
2. Alerts on account activity or passing of set thresholds
3. Monitoring of term deposits
4. Access to loan statements
5. Access to card statements
6. Mutual funds/equity statements
7. Insurance policy management
8. Pension plan management
9. Status on cheque, stop payment on cheque

### Payments, Deposits, Withdrawals, and Transfers

1. Domestic and international fund transfers
2. Micro-payment handling
3. Mobile recharging
4. Commercial payment processing
5. Bill payment processing
6. Peer to Peer payments
7. Withdrawal at banking agent
8. Deposit at banking agent

Especially for clients in remote locations, it will be important to help them deposit and withdraw funds at banking agents, i.e., retail and postal outlets that turn cash into electronic funds and *vice versa*. The feasibility of such banking agents depends on local regulation which enables retail outlets to take deposits or not.

A specific sequence of SMS messages will enable the system to verify if the client has sufficient funds in his or her wallet and authorize a deposit or withdrawal transaction at the agent. When depositing money, the merchant receives cash and the system credits the client's bank account or mobile wallet. In the same way the client can also withdraw money at the merchant: through exchanging sms to provide authorization, the merchant hands, the client cash and debits the client's account.

### Investments

1. Portfolio management services
2. Real-time stock quotes
3. Personalized alerts and notifications on security prices

### Support

1. Status of requests for credit, including mortgage approval, and insurance coverage
2. Check (cheque) book and card requests
3. Exchange of data messages and email, including complaint submission and tracking
4. ATM Location

### Content Services

1. General information such as weather updates, news
2. Loyalty-related offers
3. Location-based services

Based on a survey conducted by Forrester, mobile banking will be attractive mainly to the younger, more "tech-savvy" customer segment. A third of mobile phone users say that they may consider performing some kind of financial transaction through their mobile phone. But most of the users are interested in performing basic transactions such as querying for account balance and making bill payment.

### Challenges for a Mobile Banking Solution

Key challenges in developing a sophisticated mobile banking application are:

1. Interoperability
2. Security
3. Scalability and Reliability
4. Application distribution
5. Personalization

### Mobile Banking in the World

This part of the mobile commerce is very popular in countries where most of their population is unbanked. Countries like Sudan, Ghana and South Africa received very well this new commerce. In Latin America countries like Uruguay, Paraguay Argentina, Brazil, Venezuela, Colombia, Guatemala and recently Mexico started with a huge success. In Colombia was released with Redeban. Guatemala have the support of Banco industrial. Mexico released the mobile commerce with Omnilife, Bancommer and a private company (MPower Ventures).

## CONCLUSION

This mobile service empowers the customer with an instant access to routine queries and transactions.

### Notes and References

1. Tiwari and Buse, 2007, pp. 73-74.
2. Celent Report : According to figures published by Celent, 17 May 2007.

**15**

# *Impact of Mergers and Acquisition on Private Sector Banks in Global Economy*

M. Sumathy and M. Sathana Priya

## ABSTRACT

Mergers and Acquisitions (M & A) have been a very important market entry strategy as well as expansion strategy. This present era is known as competition era. In this era companies to avoid the competition, go for merger, and enjoys sometimes monopoly. Liberalization and technological advances are increasingly pushing the banking sector towards greater globalization to improve the operational flexibility of banks, which is crucial in the competitive environment that banks operate in. The Government also proposes to recapitalize weak banks. The recapitalization of weak banks has not yielded the expected results in the past and hence should be linked to a viable and time bound restructuring plan. The process of merger and acquisition is taken in many banks in India like— Times Bank merged with HDFC Bank, Bank of Madura with

ICICI Bank, etc. The researcher has made an attempt to measure the changes in the profitability and financial position of the above banks and has calculated several ratios and tested them in the light of 'T-test', to know the acceptance and rejection of the formulated hypothesis. The researcher has found that overall the merger and acquisition does not effect of the financial position of banks except when a weaker and non-viable banks are merged with a financially sound and profit-making banks in such case the profitability of the later banks will be affected.

## INTRODUCTION

The concept of mergers and acquisitions is very much popular in the current scenario. More so, it is significantly popular concept after 1990s where India entered into the Liberalization, Privatization and Globalization (LPG) era. The winds of LPG are blowing over all the sectors of the Indian economy but its maximum impact is seen in the industrial sector. It caused the market to become hyper-competitive. As competition increased in the economy, so to avoid unhealthy competition and to face international and multinational companies, Indian companies are going for mergers and acquisitions.

Liberalization and technological advances are increasingly pushing the banking sector towards greater globalization in which Merger and Acquisitions are both a cause and consequences. Merger and Acquisitions are considered to be fast track for increasing size. In between the two, merger has been the preferred choice for banks to grow and become big.

Basically, a merger involves a marriage of two or more entity. Merger is defined as blending of two or more entity into a single entity. The shareholders of each blending entity will become the substantially the shareholders in the entity which is to carry on the blended entity.

Merger may be taken as an abbreviation, which means:

M – Mixing
E – Entities
R – Resources for
G – Growth

E – Enrichment and
R – Renovation.

An acquisition is the purchase by one company of a controlling interest in the share capital of another existing company.

**Objectives of Merger and Acquisitions in Banking Industry**

The main objectives behind merger and acquisitions may be highlighted as under:

- To restrict competition and prevent overcrowding of banks.
- To expand market without competing.
- To gain economies of scale with less amount of investment.
- To utilize under and unutilized resources so that the banks can compete the foreign banks in global era.

**Benefits of Merger and Acquisition**

1. *For Banks*: The fruits of Merger and Acquisitions for banks are reducing unhealthy competition amongst banks, sound financial position, huge business, large assets, benefits of core banking solutions, networking and technological advancements at low cost, low cost of maintenance and human resource management, large profits, larger customer coverage. Moreover, recapitalization of weaker banks in the lights of Basel-II Norms.
2. *For Customers*: Customers are also benefited by better and faster services, competitive pricing of all products and services, increased number of branches, improved and upgraded technology, etc.
3. *For RBI*: Through Merger and Acquisition RBI is benefited by better monitoring, interaction with less number of CEOs, easy implementation of policy and convenience in surveillance due to better and updated technology, etc.

4. *For Depositors*: Depositors have better investment opportunity, negotiable environment, higher dividends, etc.
5. *For Other Related Parties*: They get Indian banks of International Standards, sound and large Indian Banks, no risk in performance of contracts and higher dividends, better and huge deals with one banks rather than two or more, etc.

### Problems in Merger and Acquisition

1. Different technology in different banks.
2. Problems in promotion, demotion, suspension and transfer of employees.
3. Management's attitude difference creates problem in management.
4. Lack of clarity of job responsibility leads to underutilized and de-motivated workforce.
5. Consolidating workforce from different working environment absentees the sense of teamwork and a shared responsibility for getting work done.
6. Difference in rationale plan for compensation and fringe benefits faces employee's opposition.
7. It will reduce flow of credit to priority sectors.
8. It will reduce competition along with competitive forces.
9. Might result in creation of "Large Financial Conglomerates" who will be difficult to supervise.

## MERGER AND ACQUISITION IN BANKING— PRESENT SCENARIO

In the LPG era, the proposal to grant autonomy to bank's board could go a long way to improve the operational flexibility of Public Sector Banks, which is crucial in the competitive environment that banks operate in. the urgency of granting autonomy is so acute that unless the public sector banks managements are given adequate powers to speedily respond to the new competitive and information technology challenges, these banks may not be viable in the long-run. The Government also proposes to recapitalize weak banks. The recapitalization of weak banks has not yielded the expected results in the past and hence should be linked to a viable and time bound restructuring plan. The process of merger and acquisition is not new for Indian banking—Times Bank merged with HDFC Bank, Bank of Madura with ICICI Bank, Nedungadi Bank Ltd. with Punjab National Bank and most recently Global Trust Banks with Oriental Bank of Commerce.

## OBJECTIVE OF THE STUDY

The main objective of the study is to measure the impact of merger and acquisition on the profitability of ICICI Bank and HDFC Bank. To make conclusion on the basis of study regarding the impact of merger on selected bank.

## RESEARCH METHODOLOGY

The data collection is very important task for the researcher. The data regarding the bank under study have been obtained from different websites and magazines. The study covers a period of 6 years in ICICI Bank before merger 3 years from 98-99 to 00-01 and after merger 3 years from 01-02 to 03-04. In HDFC Bank period of the study 6 years before merger 3 years 97-98 to 99-00 and after merger 00-01 to 02-03. For the purpose of analysis of data various ratio relating to profitability management is calculated. The statistical tools such as average, standard deviation and student's 'T'-test applied to analyze the data. The researcher has made an attempt to evaluate and measure the effect of merger and acquisition on the profitability of ICICI Bank and HDFC Bank.

In Table 1, the researcher has calculated averages, standard deviation of different ratios like return on total assets, shareholder's equity to total asset ratio, return on shareholder's fund, return on capital employed, return on investment and net profit ratio for three years before merger

TABLE I

**Analysis of Different Profitability Ratios of Banks for the Study Period**

| *Types of Ratio* | *n* | *Mean* | | *S.D.σ* | *T-cal* | *T-tab* | *Result* |
|---|---|---|---|---|---|---|---|
| | | *ICICI Bank* | *HDFC Bank* | | | | |
| *(1)* | *(2)* | *(3)* | *(4)* | *(5)* | *(6)* | *(7)* | *(8)* |
| Return on Total Assets | | | | | | | |
| Before | 6 | 0.86 | 1.72 | 0.44 | 2.39 | 2.776 | H0 |
| After | 6 | 0.89 | 0.92 | 0.40 | 0.09 | 2.776 | H0 |
| Shareholder's Equity to Total Assets Ratio | | | | | | | |
| Before | 6 | 1.66 | 4.58 | 1.83 | 1.95 | 2.776 | H0 |
| After | 6 | 0.42 | 1.22 | 0.26 | 3.75 | 2.776 | H1 |
| Return on Shareholder's Fund | | | | | | | |
| Before | 6 | 14.02 | 20.75 | 5.10 | 1.61 | 2.776 | H0 |
| After | 6 | 14.08 | 18.52 | 6.65 | 0.81 | 2.776 | H0 |
| Return on Capital Employed | | | | | | | |
| Before | 6 | 6.48 | 7.01 | 1.05 | 0.43 | 2.776 | H0 |
| After | 6 | 5.64 | 6.31 | 2.43 | 0.33 | 2.776 | H0 |
| Return on Investment | | | | | | | |
| Before | 6 | 16.95 | 17.00 | 4.69 | 0.01 | 2.776 | H0 |
| After | 6 | 17.82 | 14.25 | 7.83 | 0.56 | 2.776 | H0 |
| Net Profit Ratio | | | | | | | |
| Before | 6 | 12.28 | 21.87 | 3.04 | 3.85 | 2.776 | H1 |
| After | 6 | 14.35 | 17.80 | 2.55 | 1.65 | 2.776 | H0 |

and three years after the merger for the banks ICICI and HDFC. The different hypotheses for the T-tests are as under:

$H_o$ = There would be no significant effect of Merger and Acquisition on _________ ratio on selected Banks.

$H_1$ = There would be significant effect of Merger and Acquisition on _________ ratio on selected Banks.

$H_o = \mu_1 = \mu_0$

$H_1 = \mu_1 \neq \mu_0$

In Table 1 the researcher has calculated the T-test for different ratios. In majority of cases the calculated value of 'T' is lower than the tabulated value of 'T', which means that there is no significant effect of merger and acquisition on the different ratios showing profitability of ICICI Bank and HDFC Bank but in the case of shareholder's equity to total assets ratio and net profit ratio the calculated value of 'T' is higher than the tabulated value of 'T', that means there is significant effect of merger and acquisition on shareholder's equity to total asset and net profit ratio of ICICI Bank and HDFC Bank.

## FINDINGS

(1) There is no effect of merger and acquisition on return on total assets, return on capital employed, return on investment and return on shareholder's fund of ICICI Bank and HDFC Bank.

(2) There is significant effect of merger and acquisition on net profit and shareholder's equity to total assets of sampled banks.

# Index